HARNESS RACING
IN
NEW YORK STATE

A History of Trotters, Tracks and Horsemen

DEAN A. HOFFMAN

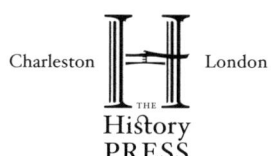

Published by The History Press
Charleston, SC 29403
www.historypress.net

Copyright © 2012 by Dean Hoffman
All rights reserved

Cover image courtesy of the Library of Congress.

All images courtesy of the U.S. Trotting Association unless otherwise noted.

First published 2012

Manufactured in the United States

ISBN 978.1.60949.604.3

Library of Congress CIP data applied for.

Notice: The information in this book is true and complete to the best of our knowledge. It is offered without guarantee on the part of the author or The History Press. The author and The History Press disclaim all liability in connection with the use of this book.

All rights reserved. No part of this book may be reproduced or transmitted in any form whatsoever without prior written permission from the publisher except in the case of brief quotations embodied in critical articles and reviews.

Contents

Preface	5
A Messenger Shows the Way	7
The Cradle of the Trotter	19
A Trotting Classic Is Born	26
A New Era Dawns in New York	38
The Fabulous '50s: New Tracks and New Races	49
Harness Racing's Mecca	61
Sire Stakes Revolutionize Breeding	76
Off-Track Betting and the Meadowlands Change Everything	91
Renaissance of Racing	99
Empire Builders	108
Sources	125
About the Author	127

Preface

George Morton Levy was on top of the world—the harness racing world, that is. That's how he must have felt as he watched the festivities and fireworks after the first Roosevelt International Trot on August 1, 1959. He could look around his dream track, built just two years earlier, and see it packed to the rafters with 48,619 racing fans. He knew that the press box was overflowing with print and broadcast media from the Big Apple and across the Atlantic. He knew that dignitaries and political leaders were in attendance.

Levy stood with a smile and accepted congratulations from well-wishers. Many had never seen a show quite like the Roosevelt International. "This is the greatest thing ever to happen to our sport," said Joe Neville, founder and impresario of the famed Little Brown Jug race for pacers.

Levy couldn't help but reflect on the opening of Roosevelt Raceway in 1940, when he and other investors brought night parimutuel racing to metropolitan New York—and lost their shirt financially. Rains delayed the 1940 opening, but the rains were a blessing because Roosevelt Raceway didn't have enough horses to put on racing. The second season at Roosevelt was better but still not profitable. And then came World War II. Racing went under a rock during the war.

Yes, George Morton Levy could look back on that night in 1959 and see how his dream had come true. Others could look back on the sport of harness racing, which had its deepest roots and greatest progenitors in the Empire State, and see how far it had come in a century. From the days of the great stallion Hambletonian, the star trotter Dexter and the first

Preface

Hambletonian at Syracuse, harness racing had come a long way in the Empire State.

What Levy and the others couldn't see that night in 1959, of course, is that Roosevelt and other New York tracks would enjoy little more than a decade of good times before new laws changed the business model for tracks. Harness racing in New York was still a viable business in the 1970s, but then it began to slip badly during the succeeding decades. Roosevelt Raceway closed in 1988, less than thirty years after that glorious night of the first International. No one could foresee that a tragedy of worldwide importance would play a role in the renaissance of New York racing, purse money would skyrocket and New York would once again become a harness racing mecca.

This book is the story of harness racing in New York, the state that can truly said to be the epicenter of the sport since the mid-1800s. Although harness racing in New York has experienced periods of both feast and famine, no other state has had a more significant impact on American harness racing.

A Messenger Shows the Way

By the rude bridge that arched the flood
Their flag to April's breeze unfurled
Here once the embattled farmers stood
And fired the shot heard 'round the world

Those were the words that the poet Henry Wadsworth Longfellow used to describe the opening act of the drama that led to the birth of the United States of America. The minutemen in Massachusetts sparked a rebellion that spread to the other British colonies in America, spurring a conflict that would last from 1775 until the improbable surrender of Cornwallis at Yorktown in 1783.

The colonists had brought a love of horse racing with them from England, but when the Revolutionary War broke out, it disrupted the importation of fine British bloodstock to the New World. When hostilities ceased, there was a rush to replenish the racing stock in the emerging American republic.

In 1788, the grey English Thoroughbred Messenger, age eight, arrived by ship in Philadelphia. After a long ocean voyage in cramped quarters, most horses—and people—were weary when it finally came time to put ashore. Not Messenger. According to legend, he charged down the gangplank so rambunctiously that it took two men to keep him under control. He stepped onto the soil of America with all the swashbuckling élan of a conquering hero. And that is exactly what Messenger ultimately became.

Messenger was just one of many English stallions that came to America. He was bred by the Earl of Grosvenor and foaled in 1780. Messenger was a son of Mambrino and believed to be the only foal of his dam. He was registered in volume 1 of the *English Stud Book*. In three seasons (1783–85) at the races, Messenger ran in fourteen races and won eight times. Nothing is known of him afterward until he arrived in America. Messenger did breeding duty in Pennsylvania and New Jersey before being relocated in 1794 to New York at the farm of Philip Platt near Jamaica on Long Island. The nomadic stallion returned to New Jersey and Pennsylvania briefly but spent most of his remaining career in New York.

The history of American harness racing is deeply rooted in New York. Due to the immeasurable contributions of horses from New York, specifically Messenger and his great-grandson, Hambletonian, the breed that started in the Empire State would ultimately spread across the continent and the world. In the sport of horse racing in post-Revolution America, Messenger's offspring proved to be extremely successful. There were few registered Thoroughbred mares in America, so Messenger was bred to any mare whose owner was able to afford his stud fee, which ultimately escalated to a high of forty dollars.

One of Messenger's daughters produced the unbeaten turf star American Eclipse, a foal of 1814 honored by the Thoroughbred industry two centuries later with the coveted Eclipse awards. Through Eclipse, the blood of Messenger shows up in countless Thoroughbred champions such as Man o' War, Whirlaway, Seabiscuit, Gallant Fox and others.

Just how did Messenger thus establish a family that developed into trotters and pacers? The exact reasons cannot be fathomed. The evolution of the American trotter took place over many decades and many generations. Perhaps the greatest clue to his influence is that Messenger's sire, Mambrino, was heralded in England as a great sire of coach horses, the steeds valued for pulling carriages and buggies on English roads. They covered the rural roads with a smooth gait that was their stock in trade.

As an individual, Messenger exhibited more brute strength than beauty when led out for inspection by visitors. He was certainly no child's horse, as his handlers had to be vigilant to avoid injury. The grey stallion was virile, fertile and able to settle many of the mares sent to him. One season he served 126 mares by natural cover. When ridden under saddle, Messenger seemed like a coiled spring. He was alert, full of energy and looking for action. He was never hitched to a buggy or cart but rather demonstrated a flashy trotting gait at times when ridden.

In 1805, when he was twenty-five, Messenger sired a bay colt that was given the name of Mambrino, the same as Messenger's sire. He was bred in

A History of Trotters, Tracks and Horsemen

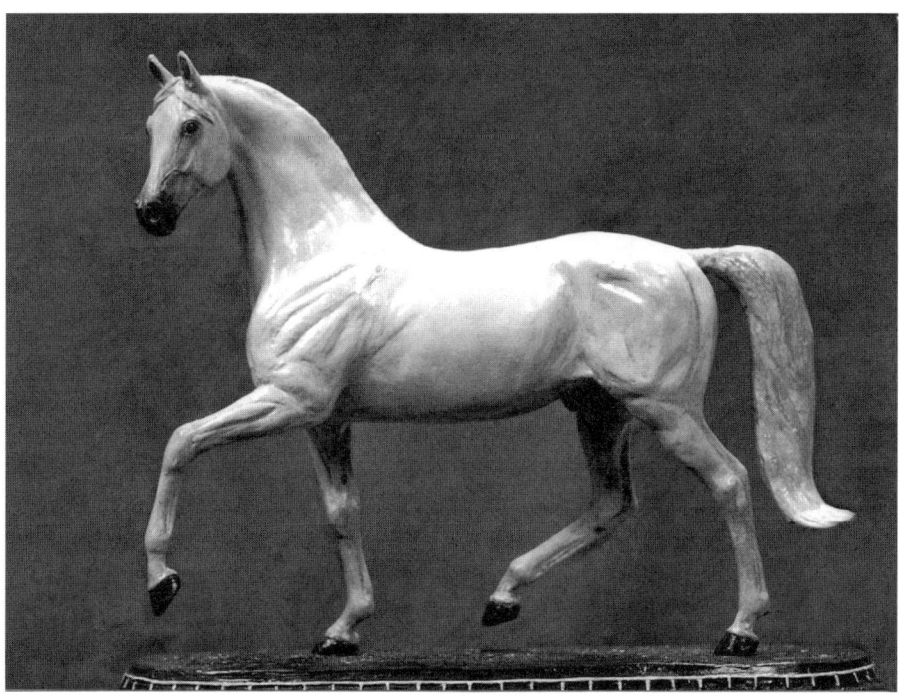

This remarkable bronze of the stallion Messenger by New York sculptor Leslie Spano was presented to author Dean Hoffman when he was awarded the Stanley F. Bergstein Messenger Award in 2005. It is the highest honor given by Harness Tracks of America.

partnership by Lewis Morris, a signer of the Declaration of Independence and later known as the "Father of the New York Turf." (Ironically, another signer of the Declaration of Independence, Elbridge Thomas Gerry, was the paterfamilias of men who also appreciated trotters and played an important role in New York harness racing. Another, Elbridge T. Gerry, born in 1908, was the first racing commissioner in the state of New York and was a partner with E. Roland Harriman in the Arden Homestead Stable. Harriman, members of the Gerry family and the Arden Homestead Stable will be mentioned in subsequent chapters.)

Messenger's son, Mambrino, ran in only one race and was defeated. He competed on a galloping, rather than trotting, gait. At age four, Mambrino entered the stud and served mares on Long Island, as well as in Orange and Duchess Counties in New York State. Mambrino was neither handsome nor fast, but he showed a trotting lick that dazzled David Jones, a respected Long Island horseman, who wrote of Mambrino, "I say with entire confidence he

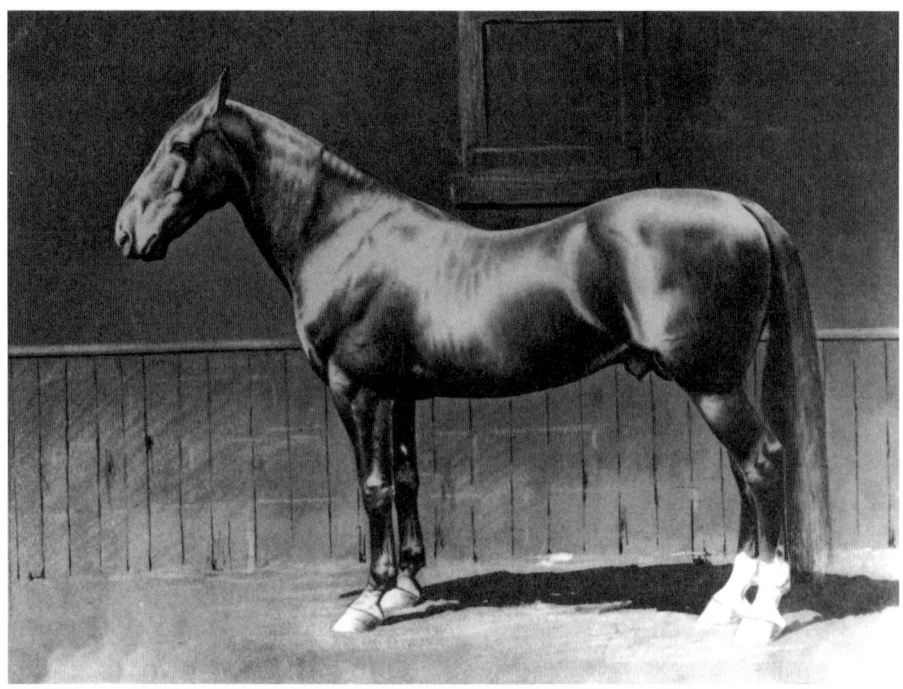

No one ever said that Hambletonian was a beautiful horse. Instead of beauty, he exuded strength and power and passed those traits along to his offspring, along with an inherent ability to trot fast. Today, virtually all Standardbreds trace their male ancestry to this foal of 1849.

[Mambrino] was the best natural trotter I ever threw a leg over…his trot was clear, square and distinct, with a beautiful roll of the knee and great reach of the hind leg."

Mambrino's lasting contribution to the breed came through his son, Abdullah, later identified as Abdullah 1 since the repetition of names was commonplace in that era before a formal registry was established. Abdullah was foaled in 1823 in Salisbury Place, Queens County, Long Island. His dam was the highly regarded Amazonia, a mare with uncertain origins but unquestionable racing ability. She reportedly was able to trot a mile under saddle faster than 3:00, a time then considered almost incomprehensible. No records were kept, and reports are sketchy, but Amazonia impressed every horseman who saw her.

In his conformation, Abdullah was his mother's son. From her he inherited a rat tail and long, pointed ears. He did not, however, have her genial disposition. He got his fervor and fire from his father's family and also was cursed with the homely and heavy head of his paternal line. As was the custom with stallions then, Abdullah was neither trained nor raced and began serving mares in New York at age three. The following year, he was briefly trained and trotted an exhibition mile near Jamaica in 3:10 under saddle, a remarkable clocking considering that he was unshod, heavy and lacked conditioning.

Breeders seeking trotters in Orange County initially rejected Abdullah as a stock horse because his offspring were high-strung and lacked the mental balance to be trained on the trot. He then stood in the New York metropolitan area and gradually gained acceptance. Horsemen eventually recognized that many of his offspring were fast and natural trotters. The ability of his sons and daughters to trot was attributed to the influence of Abdullah almost exclusively because the mares bred to him represented a patchwork quilt of obscure breeds. One of Abdullah's first standout trotters, Lady Blanche, was out of an Indian pony. That was not unusual at all in that era.

In the late 1830s, Kentucky breeder John W. Hunt was searching for Mambrino blood to upgrade his operation, and he selected the stallions Abdullah and Commodore. In the winter of 1840, the two horses were ridden the seven hundred miles from New York to the Bluegrass. Commodore arrived like a sultan and was an instant hit with breeders; by contrast, the seventeen-year-old Abdullah was injured during the trip and limped into his new home. Discerning Kentucky horsemen didn't like his looks and his lameness. He lasted only one season in Kentucky and was postmarked "return to sender."

So, in the winter of 1841, the eighteen-year-old stallion was ridden back to New York. He was so exhausted at one point that he required several days' rest before continuing to Long Island, where he stood in 1841–42. Then he made the 1843 season in Goshen in the heart of Orange County. His next home was in Freehold, New Jersey, for 1844–45. In 1846–48, he stood under the management of Ebenezer Seeley in Chester, a few miles east of Goshen.

Abdullah did not age gracefully. More than one horseman castigated him as "the ugliest horse I ever saw." His final season at stud was 1850. Thereafter, he was given to a farmer who promised to provide him with a good home for life. In 1854, the farmer reneged on his end of the deal and sold Abdullah for thirty-five dollars to a fishmonger on Long Island. He hitched Abdullah to a wagon but quickly realized the error of his ways. Despite his advanced age of thirty-one, Abdullah wanted no part of that duty and kicked the cart to pieces and broke free. The fishmonger was perhaps happy to be rid of the ugly, contrary old cuss and never pursued him.

Abdullah wandered the beach on Long Island for days, foraging on marsh grass and anything else he could find. He took refuge in a beach shanty, fighting off sand flies and mosquitoes. In November of that year, he was found dead, leaning against the wall of the shanty. It was a gruesome exit for a horse of such prominence to the emerging trotting breed.

Abdullah's importance stems from an 1848 mating to a crippled mare. The twenty-five-year-old stallion's manager, Ebenezer Seely, had a brother named Jonas who owned a seventeen-year-old mare simply called the Charles Kent Mare. She was named after a New York butcher who had once owned her. Jonas was allowed to breed to Abdullah for free. (Abdullah's advertised fee was then ten dollars.)

On May 5, 1849, Jonas Seeley gazed on his farm fields in Orange County, which were greening with the arrival of spring. He was expecting his crippled old mare by Bellfounder to foal any day now. Seeley noticed her in the distance and then spotted the outline of a foal already on its feet. The old mare had fooled Seeley, and he called to his hired man, William Rysdyk, "William! William! The mare's foaled. I can see both of them over there on the hill under the oaks. Come on!" Rysdyk abandoned his chores and joined his boss in a mad dash across the field.

The colt was already taking a few awkward steps, and Seeley appraised him carefully. This one, he told Rysdyk, was the best of the mare's five foals. "Don't you agree with me, William?" asked Seeley. Rysdyk studied the stout newborn carefully and then spoke with great deliberation.

"Mr. Seely, that's the best colt that was ever born in Orange County!" exclaimed Rysdyk. Horsemen are prone to hyperbole at times, and Rysdyk was no exception. He simply fell in love with the robust bay and soon harbored a dream to call the colt his own. The youngster matured into a stout individual that Rysdyk continued to shower with admiration and affection. He worried, however, that someone else might take a shine to the colt, someone with deeper pockets than his. Certainly Jonas Seeley was a veteran horse trader and never refused a good offer. Would he get an offer too good to refuse?

Rysdyk was just a hired hand with limited resources but unlimited dreams. He finally summoned enough courage to ask his boss if he'd consider selling the colt to him. Seeley countered by saying that he'd only be interested in a package deal: the colt with his mother. He was anxious to replace the aging, crippled mare with a younger breeding prospect. He knew how Rysdyk had his heart set on the colt, and Seeley priced the package at $150.

Rysdyk's heart and hopes plummeted. He'd told himself he might go as high as $100, if necessary, but the asking price was far beyond his reach.

A History of Trotters, Tracks and Horsemen

Seeley saw the disappointment etched on Rysdyk's face. He began thinking. His original price had a little flexibility to it, so he told Rysdyk, "Well, William, here's what I'll do and it's the best I will do. You can have the mare and colt for $125. And that's positive rock bottom. Don't try to get me to throw off any more because I don't intend to. And I'm just coming this far on your account. I know how badly you want that colt and I'm anxious that you should have him."

Rysdyk appreciated the consideration, but he was a tightfisted Dutchman who valued every dime and every dollar. He was bedeviled by his dilemma. He asked his boss if he could sleep on it. "All right, William," said Seeley. "We'll let it rest at that." Rysdyk walked into the pasture that autumn evening to gaze long and lovingly at the horse of his dreams. In his imagination, the six-month-old foal swelled in value and potential, and his faith in the colt's future grew by leaps and bounds. By the dawn's early light, Rysdyk diffidently approached Seeley and said that he wanted the mare and colt but that he couldn't pay the entire $125 at that moment. But he was good for the amount due, he assured Seeley. And Seeley knew Rysdyk's word was his bond. They shook hands. The deal was done.

That day, William Rysdyk made one of the best horse deals in history. He owned the foal, later named Hambletonian, until he died, and the stallion generated stud fees in such abundance that he made Rysdyk a very rich man and ensured the hired hand's immortality in the trotting world. When Rysdyk led the crippled mare and her playful son to his farm, he wondered what his next step should be. Should he allow the foal to mature and peddle him for a profit? Should he keep him for racing and breeding? And what about the old mare herself?

Rysdyk selected the name Hambletonian for his prize colt. It was a common name in that era. One of the best sons of Messenger had been named Bishop's Hambletonian in honor of an English Thoroughbred prominent in that period. The English horse Hambletonian was, in fact, named after the Hambleton Hills, an area in the North Yorkshire Moors, site of a racetrack for many years. To allay confusion by repetitive use of the name Hambletonian, the founder of the modern trotting breed was often called Rysdyk's Hambletonian or Hambletonian 10.

Rysdyk was so proud of the colt he had coveted from birth that he exhibited him at the Orange County Fair in the fall of 1849 and again in 1850. Fairgoers gazed at the strapping youngster with awe. He was surely some little horse! He wasn't little for long, though. He just kept growing, and by the time he was a two-year-old, he almost resembled a mature adult.

The colt hadn't been introduced to harness or a saddle, but when led next to another horse, he demonstrated a sure step on the trot. Rysdyk decided to use him as a stallion and let him cover four mares without charge in 1851 as a two-year-old.

The following year, a dispute for bragging rights about who had the best young trotting stud developed between Rysdyk and Seeley Roe, a stallioneer who was related to Jonas Seeley. Both horses served mares at twenty-five-dollar fees. Hambletonian's 1852 book encompassed seventeen mares. Roe's followers disparaged Hambletonian as a show horse without any real trotting ability, so Rysdyk had his horse broken to harness by Guy Miller and conditioned on the rural roads surrounding Chester. Rysdyk announced that he'd show off Hambletonian at the New York State Fair, then held in New York City.

Rysdyk and Roe agreed to test their horses in individual trials over the famed Union Course track, and Hambletonian prevailed with a mile in 3:03. Roe naturally wanted a rematch, and his young stallion threw down a challenge by covering a mile in 2:55.5. Hambletonian countered with a mile in 2:48.5. The time was astonishing in that era, particularly since it took years for horses to develop the physical and mental maturity to maintain such a fast trot for a mile. The fastest trotter on record then was Pelham, who had demonstrated a mile in 2:28 at age twelve. It was obvious that Hambletonian possessed a natural ability to trot fast, but would he be able to pass that along to his offspring?

It was late in the fall, and the owners were anxious to get their horses back to Orange County before winter set in. And Rysdyk knew that Hambletonian's public display of ability on Long Island would attract plenty of mares. He was right. His prize horse served 101 mares in 1853 at age four, and the following year, the owners of 78 foals paid Rysdyk a $25 stud fee. That provided Rysdyk with almost $2,000 in revenue, making his $125 investment look paltry. In these years before the Civil War, trotting was all the rage, particularly in that part of New York. Racing trotters under saddle and hitched to a wheeled vehicle was gaining popularity elsewhere, but Orange County was the heart of it all.

From the trio of foals sired when he was a two-year-old, Hambletonian got Abdullah 15 or Alexander's Abdullah. He proved to be one of Hambletonian's finest sons. In 1853, the four-year-old Rysdyk stud sired Volunteer, a stallion of monumental importance in the second half of the nineteenth century. In 1855, Hambletonian sired the champion trotting stallion George Wilkes, and in 1857, he begat Dexter, his most famous son on the track.

George Wilkes competed on the track for a dozen seasons and served notice that the times were a-changing. In a match against the famed Morgan trotter

Ethan Allen, George Wilkes slapped his rival with defeat in three straight heats. Later, George Wilkes became a stallion of immense popularity once his foals began to race and his sons entered the breeding ranks themselves. Owning a stallion by George Wilkes was later said to be "like owning government bonds."

Dexter was a gelding whose gait was so admired that he became the beau ideal of a trotter in the Civil War era. He had speed to match his stride and set records at many tracks. In 1867, he was sold for $35,000 to publisher Robert Bonner, who retired him to use strictly as a pleasure driving horse. President U.S. Grant drove Dexter and tried to purchase him from Bonner but was turned down.

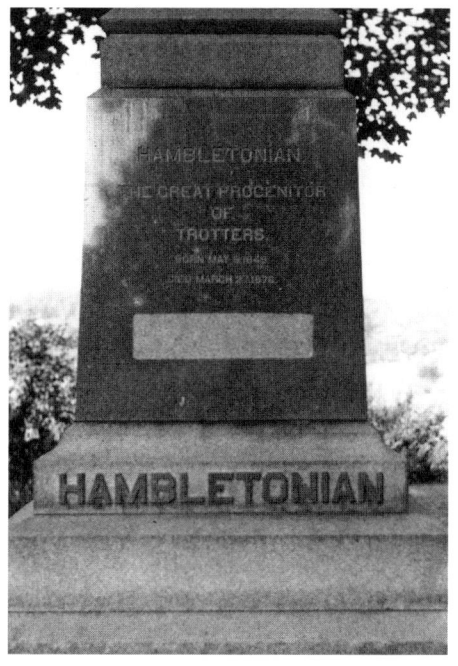

This marker in the village of Chester, New York, pays homage to Hambletonian, the father of the modern Standardbred. He was often called "the hero of Chester."

The success of Hambletonian's offspring went to Rysdyk's head. He quickly became a rich man, but like so many others in similar situations, he wanted to become even richer. He increased Hambletonian's fee to thirty-five dollars, but that didn't slow the rush of broodmares coming to Orange County. Hambletonian bred 106 mares in 1860. Even when Rysdyk jumped the stud fee to seventy-five dollars in 1863, the owners of 158 mares sent them to Hambletonian.

The engine that drove the Hambletonian bandwagon was the success of his sons, not his daughters. The males were far superior to Hambletonian's daughters, both on the track and in the breeding ranks. It was the prepotency of his male line that allows Hambletonian to live on nearly 150 years after his death.

Rysdyk was blessed that Hambletonian was a stallion of unflagging fertility. Even in his twenties, Hambletonian was able to get a high percentage of mares he served pregnant. By the latter stages of his career, however, his fee had increased to $500, a figure so high that only the wealthiest owners could afford it for their finest mares.

In the pre-Hambletonian era, trotters came from a variety of backgrounds and bloodlines; there was no discernible trotting breed. Many of the best trotters had ample amounts of Morgan, Saddlebred and Thoroughbred blood. Hambletonian changed all that. His sons burst on the scene with such radiance that he cast his competitors into the shade.

One peculiar trend developed in the post-Hambletonian era. Mares sired by Hambletonian and his sons were seldom bred back to another Hambletonian-line stallion for fear of injurious inbreeding. Ultimately, however, the dominance of Hambletonian blood was so pervasive that it was found in the male and female lines of the best trotters. It was unavoidable.

John Hervey, in *The American Trotter*, wrote that "the manner in which Hambletonian's blood was successfully inbred opened one of its principal channels of supremacy. Today [1947] we have two-minute trotters that trace to him twenty times and more—but this has been made possible by returning his blood upon itself almost exclusively by interbreeding that of his different sons whose maternal ancestry shows great diversity of origin."

It must be remembered that many of the foals by Hambletonian were never intended for competitive purposes but instead as road and driving horses. After all, that was the prevalent mode of transportation in the mid-1800s. Also, some of his best sons were seldom trained or raced, as the prevailing wisdom held that such exertion sapped their vitality for reproductive purposes.

Rysdyk was not known to turn away a mare of even the humblest origins if her owner had the cash to pay the fee. Mares thus came from a variety of backgrounds, and records of their offspring were incomplete and often inaccurate. Still, it quickly became apparent that the Hambletonian blood was an elixir of excellence for making trotters from a plow horse background. If you wanted a trotter in the years before or after America's great Civil War, you wanted a Hambletonian. It became obvious that everything else was second best.

William Rysdyk died a wealthy man in 1874, his riches coming from his bullheaded love for a colt a quarter-century earlier. It was estimated that his $125 investment returned more than $200,000 to him. His avarice was such, however, that Hambletonian paid a price for overuse. After many years of large books, Hambletonian was unable to breed in 1868, and thereafter his books were limited from twenty-two to thirty mares.

Hambletonian died two years after his owner, but his influence lived on and grew after his passing. Hambletonian blood spread from his humble home in Orange County, New York, across the United States and Canada and later crossed the oceans to advance trotting in faraway locales.

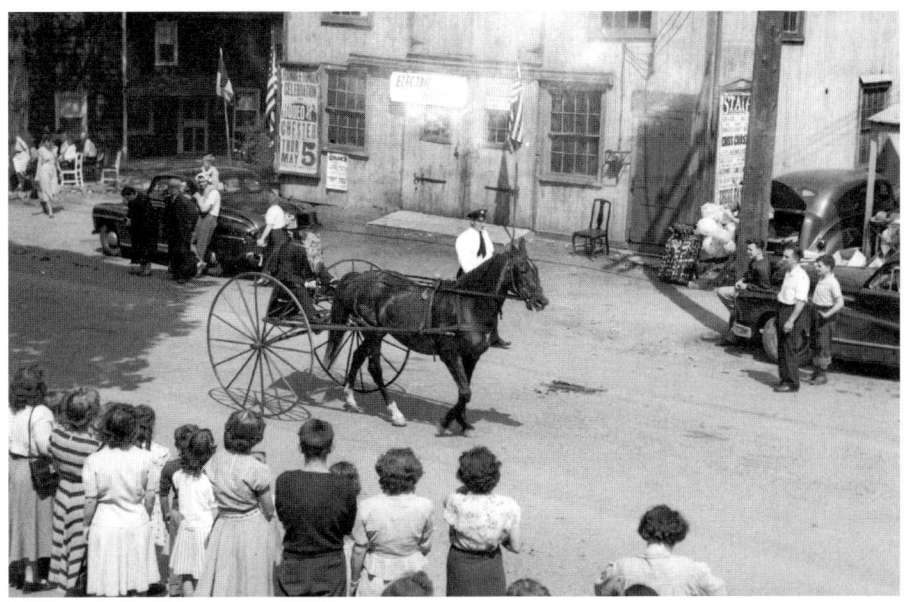

Each year before the Hambletonian in nearby Goshen, the village of Chester stages a parade to honor its famous equine resident. This entrant was dressed to represent the horse's owner, William Rysdyk.

Four sons of Hambletonian played the lead roles in carrying forth the blood of Hambletonian into the years after his death and, indeed, into the twentieth century. The first was George Wilkes, foaled in 1856 when his own sire was only seven years old. He founded what became known as the Axworthy male line in the twentieth century, principally through the 1892 stallion Axworthy and his sons, Guy Axworthy and Dillon Axworthy. This was the dominant trotting male line in the first half of the twentieth century, yielding six of the first ten Hambletonian winners, including the vaunted Greyhound. Other noteworthy trotters from the line of George Wilkes were Dean Hanover, Nibble Hanover, Titan Hanover, Florican, Hickory Smoke and Sierra Kosmos.

The pacing gait gained popularity during the march of years throughout the twentieth century, and all the trotting male lines developed pacing branches. The pacing line from George Wilkes included Knight Dream, Torpid and Vicar Hanover—the first father/son/grandson trio to win the Little Brown Jug—as well as Duane Hanover.

Two sons of Hambletonian foaled in 1863, Dictator and Happy Medium, established lasting male lines. The Dictator line developed into a pacing line that gave harness racing such stars as Billy Direct, Ensign Hanover, Tar Heel and Steady Star before waning in the final years of the twentieth century. By contrast, the Happy Medium line used the springboard of Peter the Great/Peter Volo-Volomite, another father/son/grandson combination, to dominate trotting pedigrees after World War II. From Volomite, we get Worthy Boy, Victory Song, Star's Pride, Noble Victory, Nevele Pride, Super Bowl, Balanced Image, Garland Lobell, Credit Winner and the famed "Band of Brothers"—Conway Hall, Angus Hall and Andover Hall.

There is also a pacing branch of the Happy Medium line through Volomite that includes Sampson Hanover, Bye Bye Byrd, Matt's Scooter and Somebeachsomewhere.

Scotland, a foal of 1925 and a grandson of Peter the Great like Volomite, left a legacy of trotting excellence that includes Rosalind, the filly featured in the book *Born to Trot*, and four other Hambletonian winners. His robust male line includes Rodney, Speedy Scot, Speedy Crown, Valley Victory, Muscles Yankee and Yankee Glide.

The final son of Hambletonian that carried the family legacy through his loins was Electioneer, a foal of 1868. When he was still quite young, he was selected by a group of California breeders visiting New York looking for the best available son of Hambletonian.

Once established at Governor Leland Stanford's Palo Alto Stock Farm in California, Electioneer began siring such a profusion of world champion trotters that eastern horsemen wondered what rarified air trotters were breathing in the Golden State.

Stanford detested pacers, and any horse that demonstrated a proclivity for the pace was banished from Palo Alto. So it's ironic that the Electioneer branch of the Hambletonian family ultimately became exclusively a pacing tribe. That's largely through the impact of Hal Dale, a foal of 1926. He sired Adios, Good Time and Dale Frost, and in turn, they each made significant contributions. From Adios came his son, Bret Hanover, and grandsons, Abercrombie and later Artsplace, as well as Abercrombie's successful sons. Good Time sired brilliant pacers in Best of All, Columbia George and Race Time. It was Dale Frost, however, that had the greatest influence through his son, Meadow Skipper. He is responsible for Albatross, Most Happy Fella, Western Hanover, Jate Lobell and Rocknroll Hanover.

The influence of Messenger and Hambletonian spread far beyond the borders of New York to build the breed of modern harness horses.

The Cradle of the Trotter

The Empire State was the heart of harness racing in the nineteenth century because New York City was the young nation's largest city and its business and financial center. The state of New York, of course, was far more than just the ever-expanding metropolitan area in the 1800s. Upstate, the landscape was dotted by villages and farms, and in those settings, the most common and reliable form of transportation was a driving horse. Driving horses were hitched to carriages when a farmer felt the need to go to town and were hitched to plows when it was time to till the fields. The same horse often also took the family to church on Sunday for good measure.

The descendants of Messenger and particularly those of his great-grandson, Hambletonian, were valued as driving horses because they were steady on the trot, the gait displayed by horses on the rural roads. Not only were the horses of this male line steady, but they were also fast. Just as teenagers of a century later loved to drag-race their souped-up autos, young men of the nineteenth century loved to show off their driving horses' speed on a straight stretch of roadway. Many races were started simply by one farmer boasting to another, "I'll bet my horse can beat yours to the next crossroads." And the race was on.

Driving trotters at high speed was certainly not limited to rural areas, as this was a popular pastime for city gentlemen, too. In fact, there was a stretch outside New York City known as the Hudson River Speedway where business moguls and others came to demonstrate the fancy footwork of their horses. The first documented race specifically for trotters was held in 1806, according to the New York Historical Society. It cited an article in the *Commercial Advertiser*, a New York newspaper of that era, dated June 11, 1806:

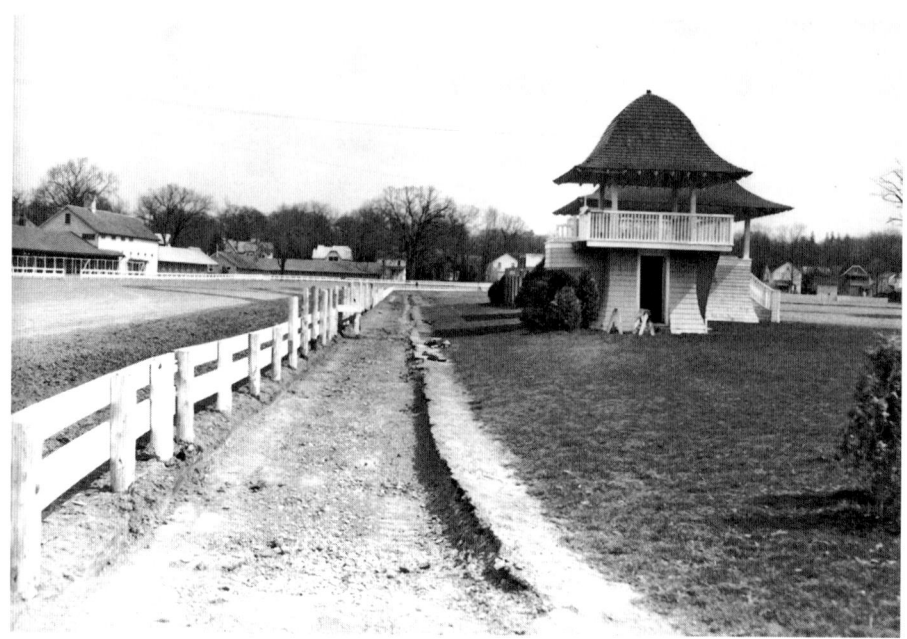

A view up the homestretch at Historic Track shows the distinctive judges' stand, which is still a fixture at the half-mile oval.

> *Fast Trotting: Yesterday after the Harlem race course of one mile's distance was trotted around in two minutes and fifty-nine seconds by a horse called Yankey from New Haven, a rate of speed, it is believed, never before excelled in this country and fully equal to anything recorded in English Sporting Calendars.*

The Harlem racecourse was reportedly located near the present site of Mount Morris Park. This is today bordered by West 118th and West 124th Streets, Adam Clayton Powell Boulevard and Mount Morris Park. New York's 3rd Avenue and Harlem Lane were other places where trotters were tested to see which one was the fastest. Tycoon Cornelius Vanderbilt and newspaper publisher Robert Bonner seldom missed a chance to sit behind their favorite steeds.

Union Course on Long Island, authorized by the New York State Assembly in 1821, was the site of the most famous Thoroughbred horse race in America two years later. It featured the northern champion Eclipse against Sir Henry, an equine hero to many in the southern states. An estimated crowd of sixty thousand people flocked to the new track to witness the grand spectacle. So many politicians wanted to attend that Congress adjourned for the day, allowing sitting vice president Daniel Tompkins, as well as Andrew Jackson and Aaron Burr, to attend the race. Eclipse was the winner after three four-mile heats were contested.

Union Course was located near the King's County Line between Jamaica and Atlantic Avenues. In the years before the Civil War, it was the site of many remarkable events featuring Thoroughbreds and horses competing on the trotting and pacing gaits. A grey filly foaled in Suffolk County on Long Island was the first trotter of national acclaim for her feats on the track. She was named simply Lady Suffolk, and she was used early in life to pull a butcher's wagon. She was said to be inbred to Messenger through both her sire and her dam, and her grey coat gave credence to that claim.

She was sold for $32.50 as a yearling in 1834 and then for $62.50 the following year. By the time she was a four-year-old, she changed hands for $112.50. She did service for a livery stable, but she was so impressive on the roads that she was given a chance to race for the first time in 1838. She was paired with Hiram Woodruff, a young man who would later achieve fame in trotting circles. In their first race, Woodruff rode Lady Suffolk under saddle in a contest with a purse of $11.00. That started a career that lasted sixteen years as Lady Suffolk raced at tracks from Boston to New Orleans. In the fall of 1845, she trotted a mile in 2:29.5 over the Beacon Course in New Jersey, the first time that a trotter had shaded 2:30. She usually performed while hitched to the high-wheeled sulkies of that era.

As Lady Suffolk's career came to a close, she was feted in song. At that time, a popular tune for children contained the chorus, "The old grey mare, she ain't what she used to be, ain't what she used to be, many long years ago." Legend has it that the "old grey mare" was Lady Suffolk herself. The old mare raced in 162 events, many of them surely consisting of multiple heats, and won 89 races.

The mania for fast trotters spread across the Empire State. Buffalo, in the western reaches of the state, had a track as early as the 1830s. It was first used for running races, but the area became a magnet for trotting devotees in the years after the Civil War. Cicero J. Hamlin purchased land outside the city in 1866 for the princely sum of $40,000 and developed it into the Buffalo Driving Park.

Hamlin knew that the best horses would follow the money, and follow they did when he offered purses up to $20,000. Fans crowded into three separate grandstands that lined the outside of the homestretch, while others crowded close to the inside rail in the track's centerfield. The judges were perched high above the spectators in a stand positioned on the inside of the track at

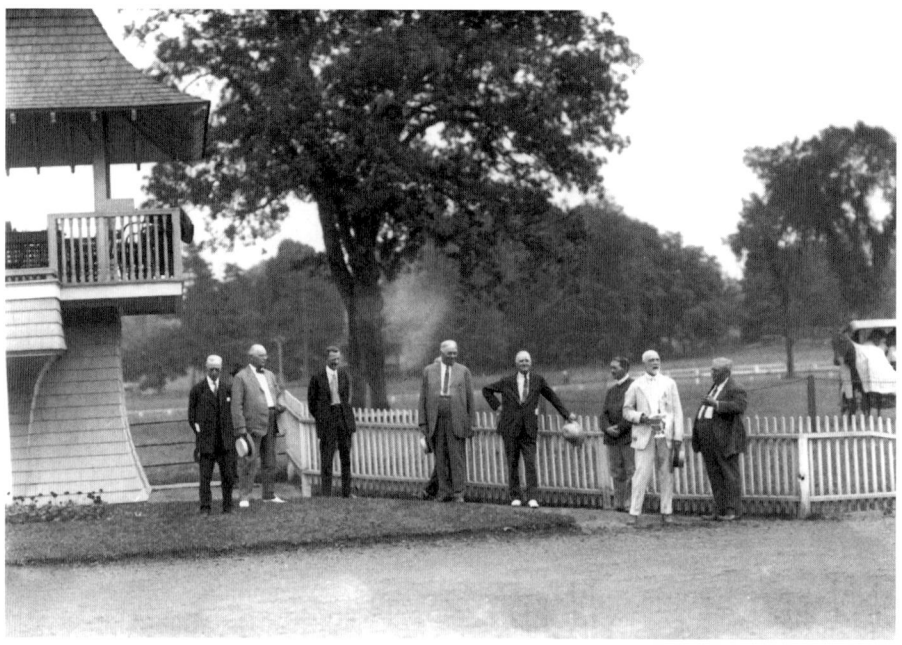

This scene at the Historic Track in Goshen, New York, shows officials relaxing between races.

the finish line. Hamlin was a promoter, and throngs of up to forty thousand people descended on the park. Following the races, the fans enjoyed three-cent pints of beer and hours of music played by the Turnverein band.

In 1871, E.A. Buck, a vice-president of Buffalo Driving Park, represented the track at a Cleveland meeting of other track operators interested in forming a circuit to provide regular racing opportunity for the best horses of that era. The following year, the same people met again at Buck's home in Buffalo. From that meeting came the Quadrilateral Trotting Combination, so-named because it consisted of a circuit of four tracks: Buffalo; Cleveland; Utica, New York; and Springfield, Massachusetts. The first races were slated for the summer of 1873.

That year, the four tracks offered purses totaling $169,300, a munificent sum in that era. But it was a time when America was enjoying post–Civil War prosperity and people were mad about their horses. It didn't hurt matters that the man in the White House, Ulysses S. Grant, was a fancier of fine horseflesh himself and loved few things more than sitting behind a dashing trotter. Grant cherished his memory of driving the champion Dexter, the greatest racing son of Hambletonian.

A History of Trotters, Tracks and Horsemen

In 1875, two more New York cities—Rochester and Poughkeepsie—wanted their trotting tracks to join the circuit, and the organization changed its named to the Central Trotting Circuit. These New York tracks were the scenes of many speed records. The mighty Dexter had lowered the world record for trotters almost two seconds at Buffalo back in 1867. Goldsmith Maid lowered the record at both Buffalo and then Rochester during her amazing 1874 season.

The Rochester track was situated at the end of a horsecar line and was opened officially on August 12, 1874. Racing lovers arrived by train from Niagara Falls, Syracuse and Buffalo. A white picket fence encircled the racing complex. When the best horses competed on the fastest tracks, the records kept falling. Rarus and St. Julien broke the speed standard for trotters at Rochester, while Maud S also seemed to love the fast mile oval in Rochester, as she lowered the trotting world record there in 1880 and again the following season.

In 1887, the tracks adopted a name that would last: the Grand Circuit. The name was indeed fitting, as the member tracks offered the grandest competition in the world for trotters. Until well into the twentieth century, all the Grand Circuit tracks were mile tracks. Any setting smaller than a mile oval was considered second rate by horsemen of that era.

The first half-mile track to be granted admission to the Grand Circuit was in Goshen, New York. A track had been established in Goshen, the Orange County seat, in 1838, and that oval—now appropriately called Historic Track—still hosts harness racing. Nowhere in New York State did the love of a trotter have deeper roots than in Orange County, located about sixty miles northwest of Manhattan. Orange County is bordered on the east by the Hudson River and on the southwest by the Delaware River, which forms the New Jersey state line. Orange was one of the twelve counties established by the Province of New York in 1683 and gets its name from William of Orange of Holland.

The United States Military Academy was established at West Point in Orange County in 1802. The county's largest cities are Middletown, Newburgh and Port Jervis, but the heart of Orange County has always been the village of Goshen. When established in 1838, the Goshen track was one-third of a mile in circumference, and trotters were exercised and raced under saddle on the track. In 1858, a larger track, a half-mile in size, replaced the original oval. The track was then known as Westcott's Meadow, and it's said that the mighty Messenger himself grazed under an oak tree that stood near the top of the stretch at Goshen. (Messenger stood at stud in Goshen in 1801.)

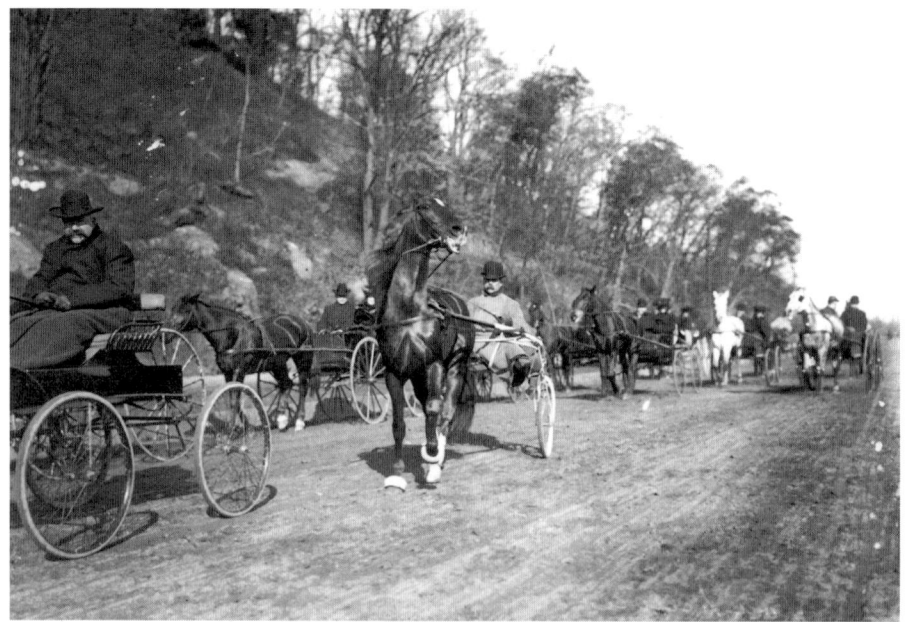

The famous trotter Lou Dillon, the first to achieve a miracle mile in 2:00 or faster, is shown on the Hudson River Speedway in New York. It was a popular place for gentlemen to show off their fast trotters.

Since many of the best trotters were bred and raised in Orange County and the surrounding areas, it was natural that they would find their way to the Goshen track. Goldsmith Maid made her racing debut at Goshen in 1865 as the nation was healing from its great civil war.

Dexter, the gelding that was the greatest racing son of Hambletonian, showcased his talents over the Goshen track with an appreciative audience that included General Ulysses S. Grant. The bearded war hero admired the champion's slashing front stroke (a gait that made Dexter the model for trotters used on weathervanes) from the loft of a barn standing along the Goshen homestretch.

In 1894, Union Pacific Railroad magnate E.H. Harriman took an interest in the events at the half-mile track in Goshen. He acquired the property and embarked on an active role in the racing and horse shows held in Goshen. That began a family participation in the sport that has spanned three centuries.

The breeding and racing of harness horses in Orange County grew during the twentieth century so that Goshen soon became know as the "Cradle of the Trotter" and also as "Trot Town USA." No one ever

A History of Trotters, Tracks and Horsemen

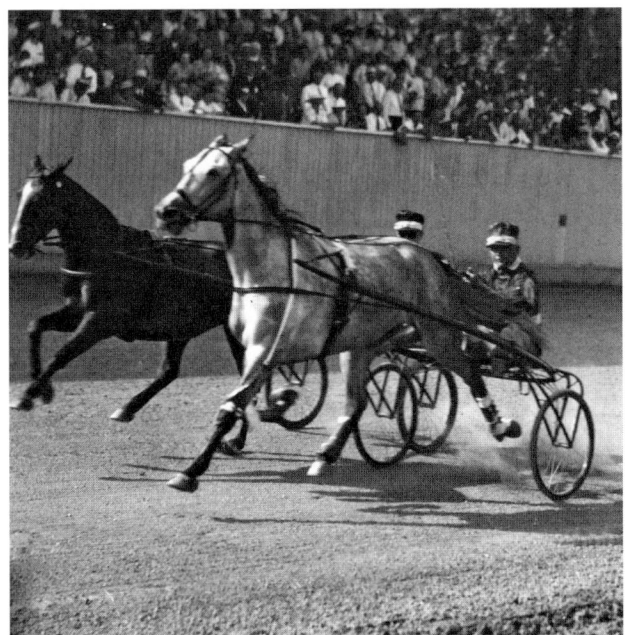

Greyhound, considered by many as the greatest trotter in the first half of the twentieth century, achieved a remarkable first when he went a mile faster than 2:00 in a time trial at Historic Track.

disputed those designations. Harness racing came to be a staple at the county fairs across the Empire State, too, as well as at the state fair in Syracuse. Farmers raced their family horses at the fairs and developed a love for competition.

As the descendants of Hambletonian and other influential sires began performing with distinction, it was obvious that a new breed of horse was in the making, a breed woven from strands of bloodlines from several other breeds. There was no breed registry, however, and no real concurrence on the standards for admission to the breed. Ultimately, it was determined that to be eligible for registration in this new breed, a horse would have to meet a certain standard of performance. To do that, a horse had to demonstrate the ability to cover a mile distance in a prescribed time. The time for the mile was the "standard" for registration, and thus the new breed ultimately became known as the "Standardbred." That term, however, was not widely used by breeders, owners and horsemen. To them, the horses were still simply "trotters," although "pacers" was beginning to make inroads in popularity.

As the twentieth century began, the horse was king of the roads in America, although a noisy, smoky, unreliable "horseless carriage" was often seen on roads, challenging the gaited driving horse for supremacy. Such scenes were a harbinger of the coming century.

A Trotting Classic Is Born

In the late months of 1923, Chicago businessman Harry Reno had a dream. He wasn't the kind of man to have small dreams; in fact, Reno's dreams often seemed like impossible dreams to others. But Harry Reno had the energy and ambition to make his dreams come true. He'd only been involved in harness racing for a short time but had already accomplished a lot. Now he thought that there should be a race for three-year-old trotters with a purse far beyond anyone's comprehension. He knew that it would increase prices for trotting yearlings and stimulate interest in breeding.

Reno enlisted the support of John Bauer, publisher of the *Horse Review*, then the most prominent harness publication. It just happened to be headquartered in Chicago. Others soon joined them, and the movement gained momentum. The first race was targeted for the summer of 1926. The planners were well into the details when they realized that they had a problem: what would they call this great race? Bauer was sitting beneath a portrait of Hambletonian, the great father of trotting, at the time. He made the connection. The new race, Bauer said, should be called the Hambletonian.

Bauer assigned his valued writer Joseph Markey to assist with the organization and promotion of the event. Markey estimated that four hundred yearlings would be nominated by the 1924 deadline and that the final purse might be as much as $74,000. As always, there were doubters. It was impractical, said some breeders and trotting publications. But Reno, Bauer and Markey were undaunted and went ahead full speed. After all, this was the Roaring Twenties; America was prosperous and happy, and the sky was the limit.

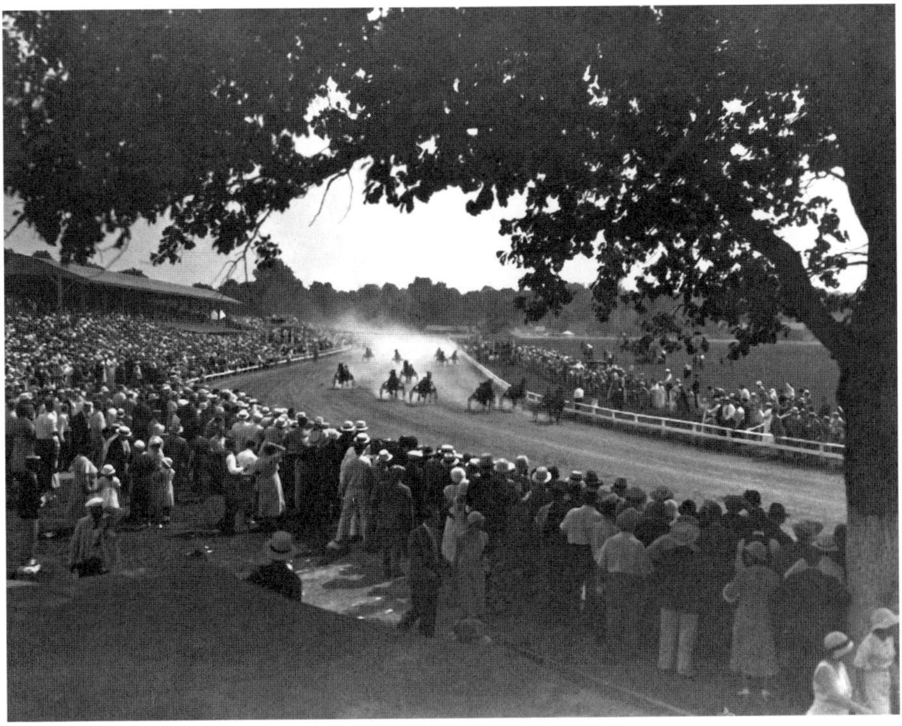

A History of Trotters, Tracks and Horsemen

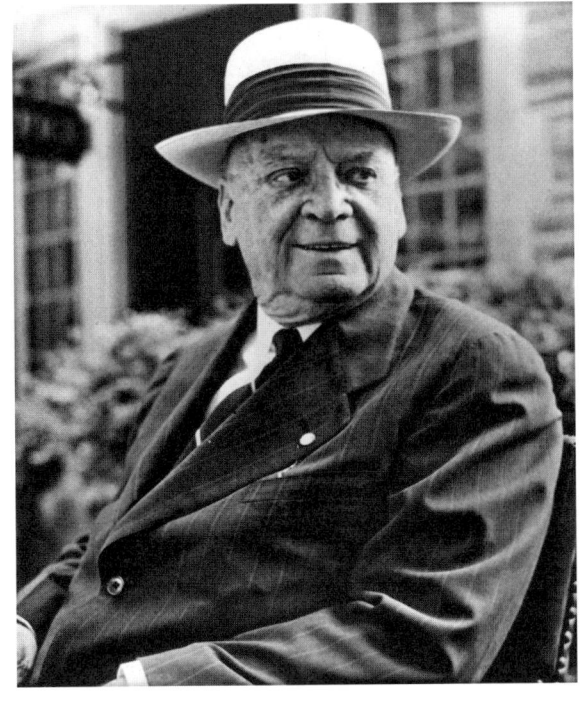

Above: This classic view of Good Time Park's homestretch is what many racing fans saw each year on Hambletonian Day from 1930 to 1956. The odd-shaped track hosted what sportswriters dubbed the "Corn Tassel Derby."

Right: William H. Cane was a hard-driving businessman who loved harness horses. He was the impresario of the Hambletonian at Good Time Park from 1930 to 1956 and also developed Yonkers Raceway into its status as the "Giant of Trotting."

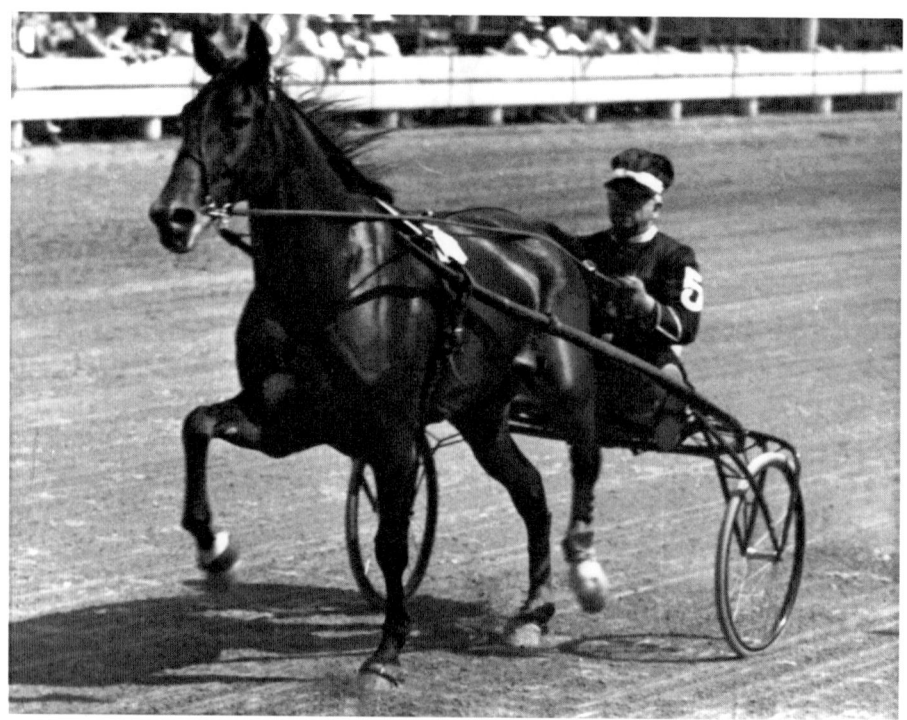

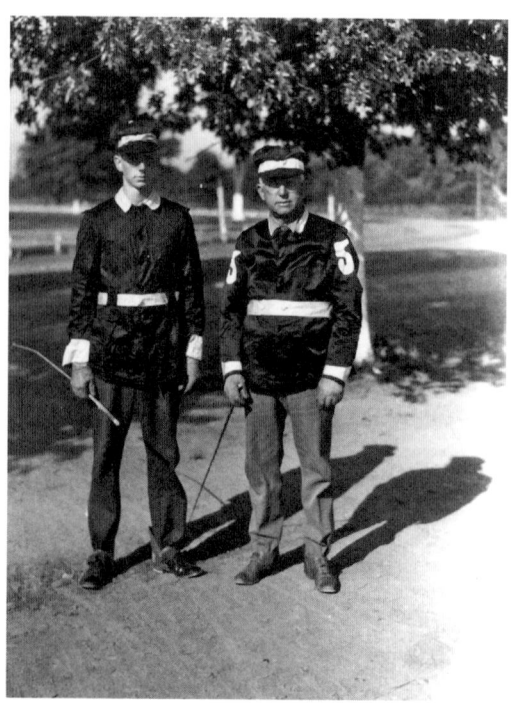

Above: Rosalind won the hearts of the American public so much that her career was captured in the popular book *Born to Trot*. She was owned by tuberculosis victim Gib White and trained and driven by his father, Ben White, who is shown with Rosalind at Good Time Park.

Left: Lanky Gib White and his father, Ben White, raced many horses in New York over the years, but their greatest moment was when Gib's filly Rosalind won the 1936 Hambletonian. The lanky youngster said, "I've got the greatest filly and the greatest dad in the world."

Where would the race be held? Cleveland's North Randall track seemed an ideal location. But other locales offered possibilities. Lexington, Columbus, Toledo, Indianapolis, Minneapolis, Springfield, Syracuse and Kalamazoo all seemed like potential hosts. The honor of hosting the first Hambletonian was put out for bids. On New Year's Day 1926, the bids were opened, and Syracuse's offer of $8,000 topped the offer from Kalamazoo.

It made sense to locate the Hambletonian at the New York State Fair because it was accessible for many of the most prominent owners and trainers of that era. It offered a spacious mile track that was ideal to test the talents of the breed's best three-year-old trotters.

The New York State Fair dates back to 1841, when the first one was held in late September in Syracuse. It was organized by the New York State Agricultural Society, formed almost a decade earlier. The fair was intended to showcase the finest agricultural products of the Empire State, and horse racing was based in agriculture and also provided entertainment for spectators. In the nineteenth century, the New York State Fair was transient, moving from city to city across the state. It wasn't until 1890 that it was permanently established in Syracuse.

The first Hambletonian was slated to be raced in early September 1926. A crowd estimated at thirty-five thousand jammed the grandstand and perimeter of the track to see history being made. Guy McKinney was picked as the obvious choice in the field, but the owners of other talented sophomore trotters weren't willing to concede anything with a grandiose purse of $73,451.32 up for grabs. The Kentucky Futurity had long been the most coveted prize for three-year-old trotters, and its purse in 1926 was only $14,000.00. The Review Futurity, sponsored by John Bauer's own publication, carried a purse of just $6,235.00.

Guy McKinney was such a heavy favorite that noted sportsman Walter Candler, heir to the Coca-Cola fortune, tried to collar him before the big race. He offered owner Henry B. Rea $40,000 for the son of Guy Axworthy. Rea, however, wanted $50,000 for his prize trotter and wasn't too anxious to sell him even at that price. Candler searched about for a suitable second choice and settled on Bronx, an impressive winner in one heat in a recent effort at North Randall. Candler ponied up $20,000 for Bronx to have a hopeful in the Hambo. He was delighted when Bronx drew post position 2 in the field of fourteen starters. To the left of Bronx at the inside rail was Guy Dean, a formidable contender, while Guy McKinney was to the right of Bronx in post 3.

Guy Dean had such a good chance of winning that his regular trainer-driver Bob Wright took himself off the colt and secured the services of crafty

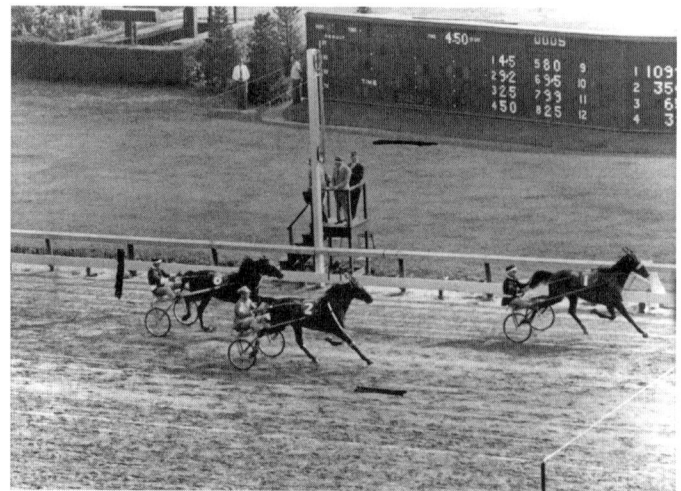

In the 1943 Hambletonian over the Empire City track in Yonkers, Volo Song won the second heat over Phonograph and Worthy Boy. The great trotter gave owner "Brooklyn Bill" Strang his second consecutive Hambletonian winner.

New Englander Walter Cox with the big money on the line. Wright felt that Cox's experience and skills would be valuable in a race with such a pot of gold at the finish line.

Hambletonian Day dawned sunny and bright in Syracuse, and the late summer heat and humidity were swept away by strong winds that would hit the horses as they traveled down the backstretch. As the trotters sprinted away to start the first heat, Cox protected his pole position and put Guy Dean on the lead. Driver Nat Ray had Guy McKinney stalking him as they braved the backstretch winds.

Once in the homestretch, with the wind at their backs, Guy McKinney came out to challenge. Guy Dean fought back gamely. Guy McKinney kept coming. Guy Dean held firm. Guy McKinney was relentless in his rush to the wire and prevailed over Guy Dean. Harness racing demanded endurance, and the rules of the Hambletonian required a horse to win two heats. So the trotters rested for an hour before returning to the track.

In the second heat, Charm, one of the four trotters from the stable of Ben White, took control early. Once again, Guy McKinney was the stalking horse, driven by Ray with confidence. Guy Dean got shuffled back to sixth place in the pack. In the stretch, Guy McKinney attacked the pacesetter. Charm offered little resistance, and Guy McKinney seemed to be coasting to victory. Suddenly, a blur appeared on the outside. It was Guy Dean, trotting unbelievably fast. With his sheepskin shadow roll and sheepskin-lined elbow boots, the colt was easy to spot in the field of trotters. Guy Dean brought the crowd to its feet. Suddenly, this race was a humdinger!

A History of Trotters, Tracks and Horsemen

Guy McKinney faltered. Walter Cox lifted the lines high to ask Guy Dean for every ounce of energy and effort. "Will he reach?" shouted the frenzied fans. Guy Dean electrified the fans with his furious attack. At the wire, however, he fell just short of victory.

"His outstretched nose was even with his opponent's throat," wrote George M. Gahagan of the *Horseman & Fair World*.

Guy McKinney's straight heat win brought owner Henry Rea a check for $45,815.92. Guy Day picked up the second-place check, while the fillies Charm and Ellie Trabue shared third and fourth money ($5,000 of the purse was paid to the breeders of the money winners). The race was hailed as a huge success by those inside the harness sport as they tossed bouquets at the dreamers who had pulled off what some people originally thought impossible.

"A new position has been gained for the racing of trotters and pacers, a plane of dignity hitherto unapproached, from which the demand may be made, without apology, for consideration equal to that offered any sport," wrote the editors of the *Horseman & Fair World* in its September 8, 1926 issue. "Ours is not a menial game, played by outlaws and mountebanks, but a great, healthful, proud sport whose hope for the future is not to rest upon an historic past but upon the forward moving procession that knows nothing short of the highest attainment."

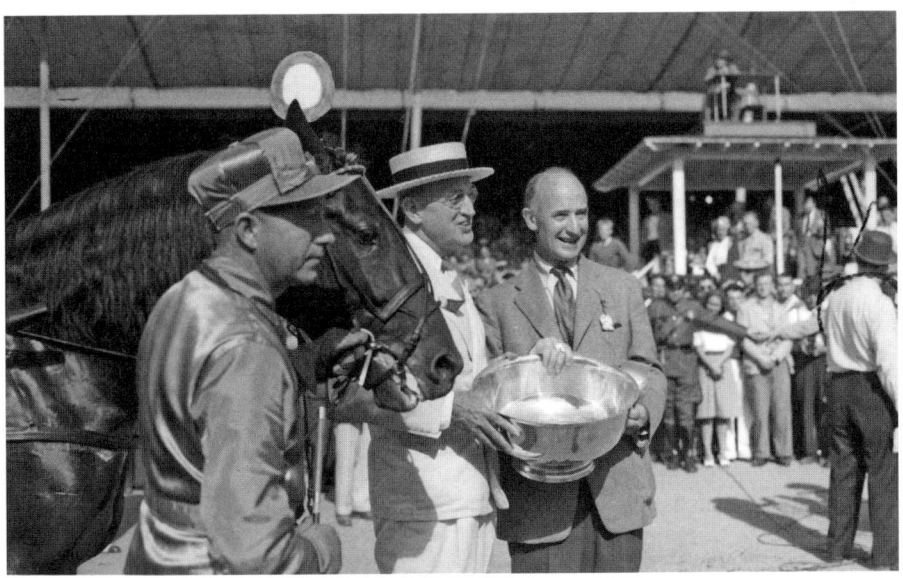

After heavy favorite Titan Hanover won the 1945 Hambletonian, Arden Homestead Stable's E. Roland Harriman and trainer-driver Harry Pownall accepted the trophy.

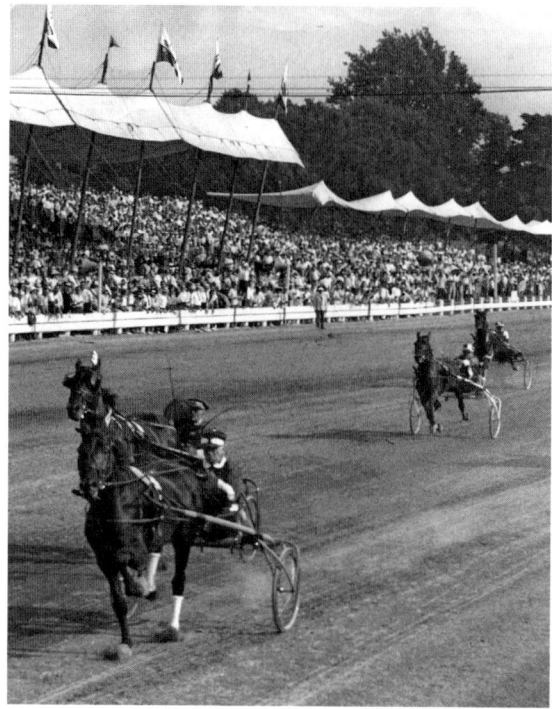

Hoot Mon trots to the wire ahead of his rival Rodney in the 1947 Hambletonian at Good Time Park in Goshen. This race marked the first 2:00 mile in Hambletonian history. Six years later, Hoot Mon made history by becoming the first Hambletonian winner to sire a Hambletonian winner when his daughter, Helicopter, won at Good Time Park.

If there was a disappointment in the aftermath of the first Hambletonian, it was that the nation's newspapers failed to appreciate the importance of the new race. They gave it short shrift in their sports columns. "The Associated Press report was sadly bungled," wrote harness journalist George Gahagan. (That failure to generate widespread media coverage proved to be a continuing dilemma for harness racing.)

Alas, the next Hambletonian was unable to follow up on the success of its curtain riser as rains pelted the Syracuse fairgrounds in 1927. The Hambletonian had to be moved to Lexington, Kentucky. It was back at Syracuse again in 1928 for a memorable race won by Spencer with a star-studded supporting cast that included Scotland and Guy Abbey. Spencer was bred and owned by David Look of New York, the first owner from the Empire State to accept the Hambletonian trophy. Once again it was rained out at Syracuse in 1929 and contested at Lexington.

After the two hit-and-miss experiences at the New York State Fair, the Hambletonian was moved to Good Time Park in Goshen starting in 1930. This famed track is now lost to history, but it was once a major stop on harness racing's Grand Circuit. It was the mile-track counterpart to the racing over the half-mile track across town at Historic Track.

The Good Time Park track was not, however, a traditional oval track with two straightaways and two sweeping turns. It might be best described

A History of Trotters, Tracks and Horsemen

as a pear-shaped track or a pyramid with rounded points. This design was in vogue during the late 1800s and early 1900s. The Good Time Park grandstand was positioned on the outside edge of the pear's right side.

Horses starting at Good Time Park had a short brush to the first turn, where they encountered a sharp left turn (comparable to the stem of the pear). That turn proved the undoing of many unsteady Standardbreds over the year. If a horse and driver weren't ready for that abrupt bend, they often forfeited their chances then and there. Those who stayed on gait through the first turn had a long "backstretch" to get settled and establish position. The horses then eased into a straight portion that formed the base of the pear before swinging into the homestretch.

The track was used for training purposes from the turn of the century until 1926, when William H. Cane, a real estate mogul and Standardbred devotee, bought the property and began conducting race meets there. In 1930, the filly Hanover's Bertha won the first Hambletonian at Good Time Park. Trotting's greatest event had found a home, where it would stay for the next twenty-six years (with the exception of 1943).

Bill Cane was a promoter, and he lavished attention on the Hambletonian to make sure that people knew about it far and wide. He also made sure that the sportswriters for the New York dailies made the trip to Goshen for what they affectionately dubbed the "Corn Tassel Derby." The second Hambletonian winner owned in New York was the Marchioness, a winner in 1932 for the widow of Ralph Keeler of Auburn, New York.

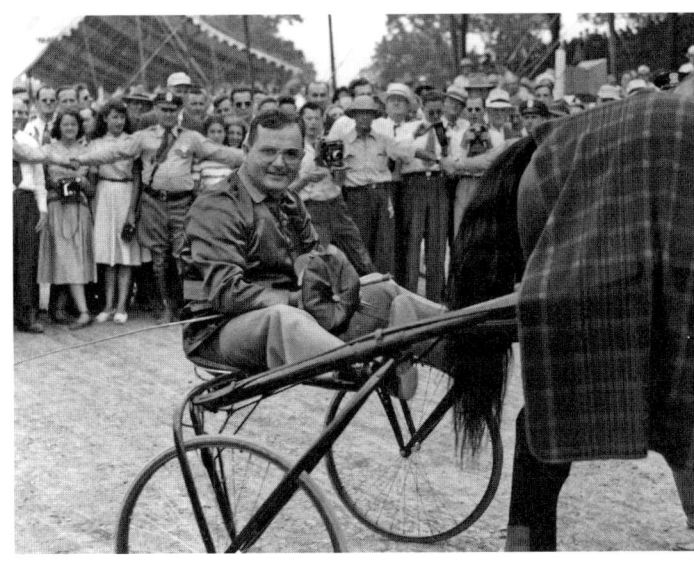

Harrison Hoyt, a hat manufacturer from Connecticut, was an amateur driver, but he made history when he won the 1948 Hambletonian with Demon Hanover.

The early years of the Hambletonian at Good Time Park, however, coincided with the start of the Great Depression. Horse racing was a diversion, not a necessity, for families struggling to put food on the table. Even wealthy horse owners were forced to cut back their stables as the business climate across America sank into the doldrums. The purse for the Hambletonian fell from $73,451 in its first year to just $25,844 in 1934. One thing that didn't suffer during the Depression was the excitement that a good trotting race generated. In 1932 and 1934, the Hambletonian fields were so well balanced that it took four heats to decide the winner. The fans at Good Time Park certainly got a good show for their money.

In 1935, they got a great show, even though the Hambletonian was decided in just two heats. That's because that star of the show, a lanky gelding named Greyhound, dominated his foes. In one heat, his surge from a trailing position to first in the long backstretch at Good Time Park was breathtaking. Spectators who witnessed it never forgot the charcoal grey gelding streaking past his foes as if they were in slow motion.

The following year, the filly Rosalind wrapped up the Hambletonian in two heats for her youthful owner, Gib White. His father, noted trainer and driver Ben White, had given the boy this filly to help the youngster overcome his bout with tuberculosis. She blossomed into a talented girl capable enough to beat the boys, and that's exactly what she did on Hambletonian Day. Young Gib hugged his father after the race and told spectators and that he had the best filly and the best father in the world. No one disagreed.

One of the most prominent owners in the trotting world in this era was William H. Strang Jr., a genial man known as "Brooklyn Bill" to his many friends in trotting. His quest was to win the Hambletonian, and he seldom failed to send one of his horses to the post in the Hambletonian at Good Time Park. The winner's circle, however, proved elusive for Strang. In 1937, Strang's filly Twilight Song got a small piece of the Hambo purse, and two years later, the Abbot, owned in part by Strang, earned a nice check for his 4-4 finish.

In 1940 Strang's filly Queen Victoria earned fourth money in the Hambletonian, and the following year, his colt His Excellency won the first heat before dropping the next two to Bill Gallon. Strang's dream of clutching the Hambletonian trophy seemed to be increasingly elusive. In 1942, however, Strang's Hambletonian dream came true when the Ambassador, a long shot in the field of eleven, scored a major upset. The Ambassador paid $68.20 for a $2.00 bet in winning the second heat and took the third heat over Scotland's Comet to earn the trophy for a jubilant Strang.

A History of Trotters, Tracks and Horsemen

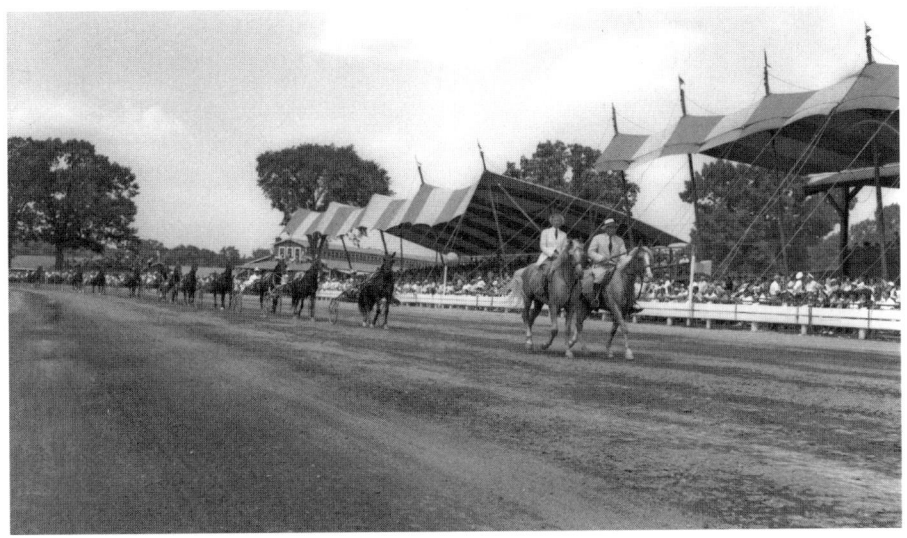

Hambletonian Day at Good Time Park was always a festive highlight of the New York racing scene. This image shows the Hambletonian starters being paraded to the post by outriders and fans getting a close-up look at their favorites.

After the post-race excitement subsided, Strang walked into the office of race secretary Al Saunders. He asked Saunders to cash a large personal check, which was done. After all, Strang had a check of $20,489 coming as the winning owner. That gave Strang "a sheaf of bills that would not go in the pocket of a plasterer's apron," according to one observer. Strang walked down the line handing each of Ben White's caretakers a bill that would buy a small piece of property in the area of Lexington, Kentucky, where many of them lived. He also gave Guy Heasley, the efficient bookkeeper and master of transportation of the Ben White Stable, a substantial check. It was customary to give a trainer-driver 10 percent of the purse winnings, which would have given Ben White $2,048. Strang instead wrote White a check for $5,000. This incident demonstrates what kind of guy Brooklyn Bill Strang was, and it shows how much winning the Hambletonian meant to him.

In the summer of 1943, wartime restrictions on gas and tires curtailed travel, and the Hambletonian was moved to the Empire City track in Yonkers. The harness horsemen weren't happy with the deep footing on the Empire City surface. In the first heat of the Hambletonian, the heavy pre-race favorite, Volo Song, owned by Bill Strang, went offstride as Worthy Boy shrugged off his soreness to win the opening round. Volo Song rebounded to win the second and third heats to give Strang his second Hambletonian trophy in as many years.

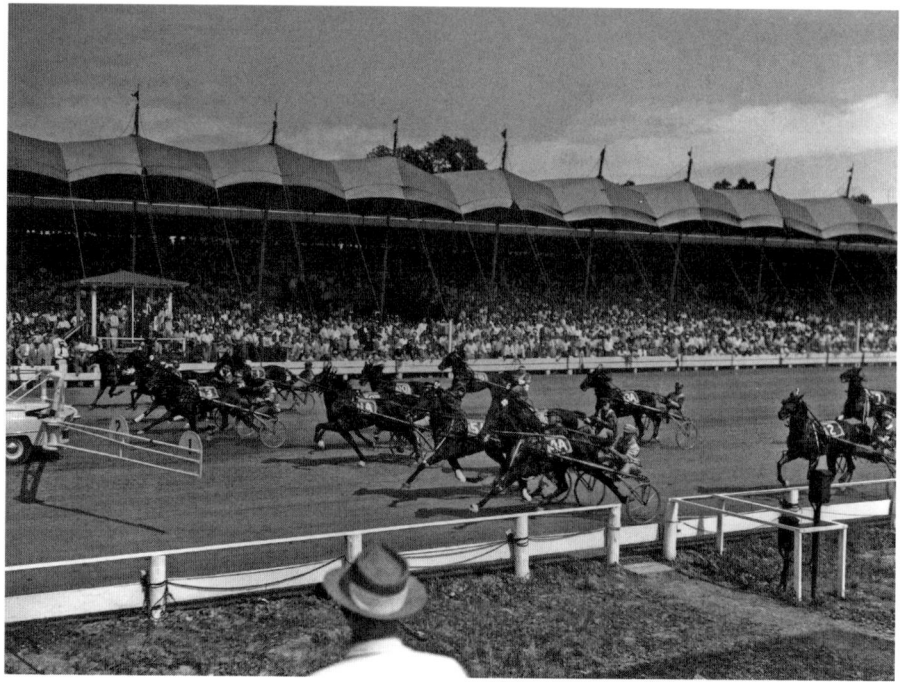

The starts of the Hambletonian and other races were greatly improved by the Steve Phillips Starting Gate. This shows a large field getting underway at Good Time Park.

A galaxy of Standardbred stars stepped over the Empire City track during that 1943 meet while war was raging across the oceans. In addition to Volo Song and Worthy Boy, the luminaries racing at this Empire City meet included Adios, Bill Gallon, Love Song, Scotland's Comet, the Colonel's Lady and His Excellency.

In 1945, Titan Hanover was such an overwhelming favorite in the Hambletonian that he was barred in the betting. He started from post position 12 on the outside of the second of three tiers of nineteen starters. The bulky field didn't deter the little package of dynamite from dominating the field in two easy heats. Titan's victory was extremely popular because he was owned by Arden Homestead Stable, a partnership of E. Roland Harriman and Elbridge T. Gerry, both from New York. Harriman had invested considerable sums to support the trotting sport over many decades; he was also was widely credited with saving harness racing when he organized the United States Trotting Association in the late 1930s. Gerry was his nephew and the first racing commissioner of New York State.

A History of Trotters, Tracks and Horsemen

The Hambletonian at Good Time Park always provided drama of varying kind. In 1947, Hoot Mon trotted the first mile in 2:00 in Hambletonian history in his epic victory over his rival Rodney. A year later, hat manufacturer Harrison Hoyt made history when he became the first amateur driver to win the Hambletonian.

In that era, big fields were prevalent in stakes events, and the Hambletonian was no exception. In 1953, twenty-three colts and fillies lined up behind the starting gate in search of the big prize. Helicopter, a filly from the first crop sired by Hoot Mon, broke stride and finished seventeenth in the first heat but came back to win the second and third heats. She was the first Canadian-owned Hambletonian winner, and she was the first Hambo winner sired by another Hambo winner.

Not everything was rosy in New York racing, however. In 1953–54, an investigation into New York harness racing under the state's Mooreland Act Commission tarnished the reputation of racing and resulted in an onslaught of negative coverage in the state's newspapers.

In the mid-1950s, a rift between New York racing commissioner George Monaghan and the United States Trotting Association cast a pall over the extraordinary success the sport was enjoying. It was essentially a dispute over which organization had jurisdiction over racing in the Empire State. Would it be the U.S. Trotting Association, a national organization based in Ohio, or the state-sanctioned New York State Racing and Wagering Board?

Commissioner Monaghan felt that New York should govern parimutuel activities within the state and should be the proper governing body to establish rules, issue licenses to participants and oversee the conduct of the races. The dispute caused so much dissatisfaction and alarm within the harness racing community that the directors of the Hambletonian Society expressed concern about the conduct of the classic trotting event in the Empire State. There was also concern about the future of racing at Good Time Park as owner William H. Cane was in declining health. This led to the transfer of the Hambletonian in 1957 from New York to the Du Quoin State Fairgrounds in faraway southern Illinois. It was a blow to the prestige of New York racing.

The dispute over sovereignty between the state racing regulators and the U.S. Trotting Association simmered throughout the remainder of the 1950s. State officials saw themselves as partners with the national organization in governing harness racing, but state commissions ultimately gained the upper hand. The U.S. Trotting Association continued to promulgate rules, but when its rules differed from state rules, the state's racing rules always superseded USTA policies.

A New Era Dawns in New York

The race meet that changed harness racing forever almost never happened. It certainly didn't happen as planned. In 1940, some cockeyed optimists on Long Island put their full faith and credit into an experiment unlike anything harness racing had ever seen. It would be a thirty-day meet over a half-mile track in Westbury. The programs would be held at night under the lights, and the grandstand proposed would optimistically accommodate eight thousand people. A horseshoe-shaped paddock with sixty-six stalls was built at the first turn. Betting would be conducted on the parimutuel basis, eschewing the bookmakers found at many other race meetings of that era. Racing would be held every night except Sunday from August 26 to September 30.

"The outcome at Westbury will be watched with deep interest by many, even those denied the chance of being personally on hand for this novel racing enterprise," wrote *Hoof Beats* in an editorial. "Behind the project are a group of real sportsmen who have faith in the love of a sufficient part of the metropolitan center to make up a fine return income from racing attendance, and it is the intention of those to leave nothing undone to make this enterprise one with an appeal that will accomplish the end that is desired by all true sportsmen."

The new track would be called Roosevelt Raceway. All that was needed to make the opening night successful was horses. But they didn't come. What did come was rain. Day after day of rain pelted Long Island and forced the postponement of the opening night of racing. In that era, racing surfaces were mostly clay, and they quickly became quagmires when wet. After so much fanfare, the letdown seemed enormous.

A History of Trotters, Tracks and Horsemen

As bad as the rains were, they were also a blessing. Few people knew that Roosevelt Raceway didn't have enough horses to fill races on its opening night. Officials put out an appeal to owners and trainers, but the plan of having full fields for eight races at night, six nights a week, suddenly seemed an impossible dream. The rains bought Roosevelt Raceway time. Officials redoubled their efforts to lure horses to Long Island, imploring horsemen that the success of this experiment (and their considerable investment) was in jeopardy.

When the races finally got underway on September 2, 1940, the horses came, and so did 4,584 patrons. The winner of the first race was the mare Matha Lee, later to be the dam of the influential New York sire Greentree Adios. The pathway to a parimutuel meet at Roosevelt Raceway had been paved by legislation sponsored by John J. Dunnigan, a state senator for twenty-nine years. In the 1930s, Dunnigan repeatedly introduced legislation to replace bookmakers with parimutuel betting in the Empire State, but the parimutuel bill wasn't passed until 1939. Before Roosevelt opened, a Thoroughbred parimutuel meet at Jamaica had opened on April 15, 1940.

Roosevelt Raceway's first meet closed on October 5 when 3,900 people pushed through the turnstiles and bet $70,020. The delayed opening was successful and closing night rewarding, but for too many nights in between, the crowds were sparse. People didn't come in sufficient numbers to make the venture profitable.

It was estimated that the Roosevelt Raceway partners lost $100,000 that first season, a setback that would have sent most ventures into bankruptcy. But George M. Levy and his partner Bob Johnson weren't the kind of men willing to cut and run. They swallowed their losses and continued to preach optimism so fervently that they convinced others that the Long Island experiment would succeed. They talked and promoted and then talked and promoted some more. They also planned for the future. They announced that they would invest an additional $100,000 to update the plant before the 1941 meet. The lighting system needed to be refined, and roads needed to be paved within the plant. Barns were built. Listeners were impressed. These men had staying power, they whispered. They were in business to last.

Although George Morton Levy gets and deserves much of the credit and recognition for Roosevelt's ultimate success, the role of Bob Johnson cannot be overstated. He came from an Ivy League background and was a sportsman with many connections in the New York area. He was a broker with E.F. Hutton on the New York Stock Exchange. Johnson didn't have an extensive background in the trotting world, so he wasn't quite sure what he

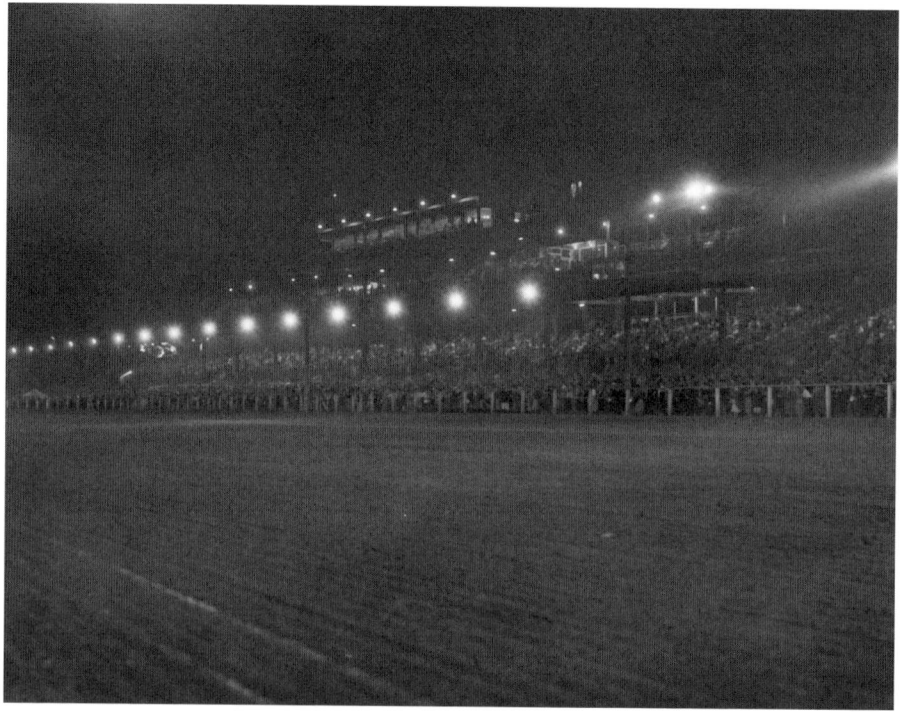

This early shot of Roosevelt Raceway, a pioneer in parimutuel racing, shows how crowded the grandstand was despite lighting that was dim by modern standards.

was getting into at Roosevelt, but he came away impressed. He particularly liked the competitive spirit of the drivers. "I have never met up with a more cooperative bunch of fellows in any sport," he said. "I've heard a lot about the contrariness of drivers in this game, but I assure you it was all a surprise to me; they were swell."

Other racing devotees watched the much-ballyhooed Roosevelt "experiment" with interest and with a belief that it could be duplicated in other markets. With far less fanfare than Roosevelt Raceway, a betting meet opened three weeks after Roosevelt in the fall of 1940 in Batavia, New York. The idea for a parimutuel meet at Batavia started in the summer of 1939 when William (Lefty) Goldberg spotted a story in a New York newspaper that the New York General Assembly had given the green light to a constitutional amendment allowing parimutuel wagering. It needed statewide approval from voters, but Goldberg was confident of the outcome.

Goldberg was known to risk a few dollars on a horse race himself, but he was a shrewd enough businessman that he knew that a lot of dollars could be made by getting in on the ground floor of this opportunity. He met with state senator George Manning in Rochester, and they applied for a track license. He had already made arrangements to lease the Genesee County Fairgrounds for his meet. The new meet paid a fee of $100 per day and underwrote the cost of the necessary improvements to open the new Batavia Downs.

The track in Batavia would offer thirty days of racing with a $500 minimum purse, each race two dashes and with no entrance fee. The track was less than a half-mile track, so two laps were still sixty feet short of a mile. The races had to start and stop in different places, and timers had to click their stopwatches at the proper moment.

Batavia opened on September 20, 1940, and the first race went to Rip Harvester in 2:14-3/4. The first race betting pool came to a grand total of $629. Attendance that night was estimated at 2,500, and they bet $10,411. Early in the meet, Duke of York set the track record at 2:07-3/4. The pioneer meet ended three days early because of "poor patronage blamed on unfavorable weather," according to a local newspaper. The backers of Batavia Downs lost money. But it was a start.

In the big picture of harness racing in the fall of 1940, the debut of racing at Roosevelt and Batavia did not make a great splash in the sport's periodicals. The harness world was caught up in the battles on the Grand Circuit. At Indianapolis, Spencer Scott and Bill Gallon looked like the best trotters in their age group, and a young Pennsylvania horseman named Delvin Miller won the Fox Stake with Blackhawk. With a purse of $14,920, the Fox Stake was then the richest race for pacers.

While the meets at Roosevelt and Batavia were greeted with enthusiasm by horsemen, one segment of the sport that wasn't so eager to embrace the parimutuel plants with open arms were the fairs in New York that conducted harness racing. They argued before the New York Harness Racing Commission that the city tracks with extended meets were going to deprive them of the horses needed to conduct fair racing. Several fairs asked that dates not be given to the new tracks for 1941 as they were undermining county fair competition. New York Harness Racing chairman Elbridge Gerry handled the situation with diplomacy, pointing out that there was a large enough horse population to provide racing stock for the fair meets and the extended meets. Besides, he reasoned, competition for horses could only be good for owners and trainers and give them more opportunities to race.

The fairs weren't the only ones keenly aware of what was happening on Long Island and in western New York. Harness horse devotees in the

Saratoga area felt that they could capitalize on the deep horse traditions in that area with a raceway meet. The site they picked was the farm of horseman W. Ellis Gilmour, which already had a half-mile track that Gilmour had used for training and matinees. Soon, 107 acres were converted into a modern racing plant in the spring and summer of 1941. The location was formerly part of the Harry Payne Whitney estate, and it was adjacent to the famed Thoroughbred track where races had been contested for three-quarters of a century. The question that locals and so many others in the Empire State asked was whether the sulky sport could gain favor in a locale with such deep roots in the Thoroughbred world.

Gilmour partnered with local attorney Frank Wiswall, and then Dunbar Bostwick, treasurer of the U.S. Trotting Association, joined them. Soon, E. Roland Harriman, who operated Arden Homestead Stable, added his name to those pushing the idea of a parimutuel raceway. They hired Milton Danziger as the general manager of the embryonic enterprise. Danziger literally lived at the Saratoga track as it was taking shape, supervising every detail of the construction and hiring a team that would be ready on opening night. Saratoga was blessed with perfect weather that allowed the construction to proceed at a rapid pace. The steel and concrete Saratoga grandstand had a pressroom and photo finish booth perched on its roof.

The perfect weather disappeared, as luck would have it, once the opening night of June 26 neared, but the first night of competition at Saratoga went on as scheduled, and racing continued through the end of July. The first season was deemed to be a success, and officials began looking ahead.

As Roosevelt Raceway prepared for its second meet opening in May 1941, its training roster included Will Caton, Jimmy Jordan, Delvin Miller, Wayne Smart, Gene Pownall, Allie Cornwell and others. Before Roosevelt opened the 1941 season, management felt obligated to quell rumors that small stables had no place at the Long Island track. "There is no desire on the part of the association to discourage the small man," said a track press release. "Instead every effort will be made to encourage him and give him every possible opportunity. The existence of the Grand Circuit racing at Westbury with its attendant large stables will not alter the policy of the management in affording opportunities for the small man to start his horses in races where such horses belong. The association realizes keenly the importance of the small racing stable, also that the small man is the backbone of the trotting sport and everything will be done to encourage him at the Westbury meeting."

Once the track was opened for business in the spring, the weather turned inclement. George Levy decreed that the show would go on unless the rains made it absolutely impossible for horses and men to stand on the track. He was tired of Mother Nature raining on his post parades at Roosevelt. The heavens continued to drench Roosevelt, though, during the first night of racing, but that didn't dampen the spirits of the 3,665 people attending; they bet $57,000.

When the weather cleared, the widely admired war horse pacer Little Pat went an exhibition mile in 2:05, which broke the track pacing mark and tied Nibble Hanover's track mark for trotters. That mark didn't last long as Stoneridge Direct, a recent refugee from pulling a wagon in Pennsylvania's Amish country, zipped to a 2:04-3/4 mile.

On July 2, Gilt Hanover won and paid $239.60 for a $2.00 bet. The seventeen lucky ticket holders shared their good fortune by spreading the word about Roosevelt Raceway. "Hey, buddy, you can make a small fortune betting the trotters" was likely a comment that spread among sports lovers. Such word-of-mouth advertising was the best possible endorsement for a business.

The 1941 meet was much like the first Roosevelt Raceway meet. The principals stayed the course, counting on a brighter day down the road. They were vindicated when the final night of the 1941 season had the largest crowd. When the first meet of 1941 ended after thirty-three nights of competition, more than $90,000 in purses had been distributed, and the average purse was $377, a significant sum in that era. Some 127,000 people attended the races and bet a total of $2,450,00, giving Roosevelt an average handle of $70,000 (versus a $44,000 in 1940).

Roosevelt passed the test. It passed the test from patrons, who found it comfortable and modern, a far cry from the wooden grandstands and dusty tracks where they'd witnessed harness racing in the past. It also passed the test with horsemen because of the purse levels and facilities for horses and those who managed them.

Levy and Bob Johnson were the driving forces behind Roosevelt, but they didn't make these miracles happen alone. Al Saunders was the race secretary, and the team of judges included John A. Cashman, a figure of great importance in Roosevelt's future and the father of a Hall of Famer with extensive influence in harness racing later in the century. The second season of thirty nights at Batavia also showed promise for sustaining a parimutuel meet in western New York.

Just as Roosevelt, Batavia and Saratoga were looking forward to improving fortunes in 1942, the Japanese attack on Pearl Harbor thrust America into World War II and changed the landscape of American life and business. Suddenly the racing of Standardbreds didn't seem so important.

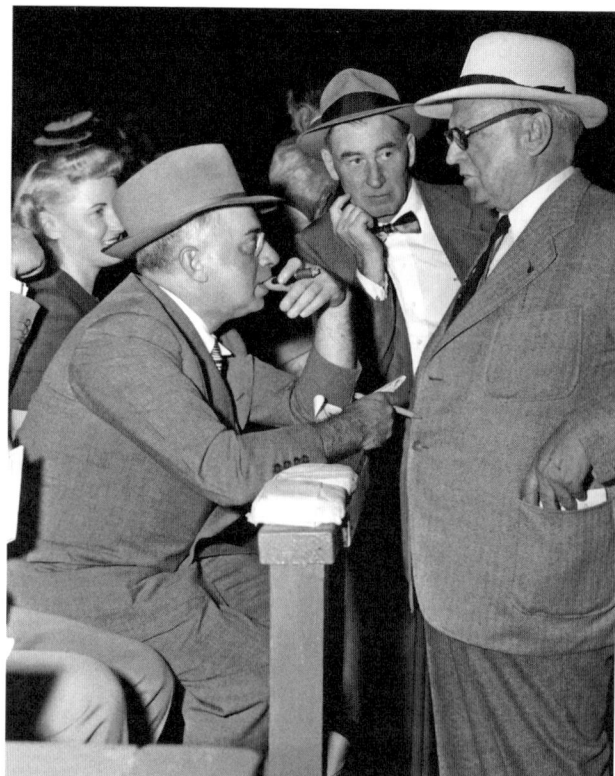

Three titans of the early years of New York parimutuel racing are, from left to right, George Levy, Robert Johnson and William H. Cane.

In 1942, Roosevelt's meet was moved to a 5:30 p.m. post time because of wartime restrictions on lighting. Still, both Roosevelt and Saratoga hosted Grand Circuit racing in 1942, a testimony to how highly they were regarded in the harness world. In fact, the Fox Stake, the richest pacing race in the world, was moved to Saratoga when the Indiana State Fairgrounds was taken over as a base by the U.S. Army. When the Grand Circuit racing opened at Saratoga that summer, among the drivers seen in the sulky were Henry Thomas, H.M. Parshall, Clint Hodgins, Lee Smith, Rupe Parker, Wayne Smart, Harry Pownall, Harry Whitney and Delvin Miller. A youthful speed sensation named Adios won the $15,840 Fox Stake despite demonstrating an alarming ability to put on the brakes late in his races.

In western New York, Batavia Downs floundered during the war years and didn't attain solid footing until after the war ended. A new track in the Buffalo suburb of Hamburg made its debut in the spring of 1942. The timing hardly could have been worse. Much of the potential customer base was in uniform and far from home. It was simply a terrible time to start a business that was basically recreational at heart. In 1943, Roosevelt's racing dates were moved to the Empire City track in Yonkers. Saratoga's meet was held there, too, as were the racing dates allocated to Buffalo Raceway. During the war years, horse racing was strictly an afterthought as so many horsemen and racing officials were called into the service of Uncle Sam.

Night racing returned to Roosevelt Raceway on May 29, 1944, about a week before Allied troops stormed the beaches at Normandy in their invasion of northern Europe. By this time, the tide of the war had clearly turned; many people thought that the fighting would be over and that the boys would be home from Europe by Christmas. After no racing at Roosevelt in almost two years, fans were ready for some action. Some 7,800 attendees poured $220,034 through the parimutuel windows.

World War II came to a close in Europe in the spring of 1945, yet the war in the Pacific raged on. The Japanese vowed to fight to the finish, and Allied commanders feared a bloody battle on the beaches if an invasion of Japan were necessary. The use of atomic bombs in August obviated the need for land-based combat in Japan. The formal surrender took place on September 2, 1945. This meant that it wouldn't be long before the American soldiers would exchange their uniforms for street clothes and make the long-awaited transition to civilian life. With that transition came an explosion in the popularity of harness racing as Americans found that going to the races was a great way to spend an evening.

One of the stumbling blocks in these early years at the parimutuel plants was the fact that harness races suffered from ragged, uneven and often unfair starts. The drivers were tasked to bring their horses to the start, fanned out across the track in post position order. The one inviolable rule was that no horse was to have its nose ahead of the pole (or inside) horse when the race began. Such a system relied on the cooperation and sportsmanship of the drivers, but what competitive driver was above taking a little edge if it improved his chances of winning?

Starting judges could be tyrants and were empowered to mete out fines and suspensions to drivers breaking or even bending the rules. But getting a fair start often took several tries, and the delays certainly tried the public's patience. Starting harness races from a standstill, as was done with Thoroughbred races, was not practical, though it was done at times. Everyone agreed that the fairest start would be one with all the horses moving in unison, but how could fairness be achieved?

Various mechanical methods of starting races were tried in the early 1940s. They went by such as names as the Phantom Barrier, McNamara Barrier and the E.M. Smith Starting Gate. The latter consisted of a barrier of metal cables that stretched across the track. It was controlled from a small car that ran on rails just inside the hub rail. All of these methods had their merits and their supporters, but Ohioan Steve Phillips felt that the best way was to mount folding wings on the back of an automobile. Many scoffed at the idea of using an automobile to start horse races. Would the horses spook when they saw it on the track? What if the car stalled or if the wings failed to fold? Phillips was aware of the objections, but he kept tinkering with his contraption to work out the bugs and to make it acceptable. Many horsemen weren't convinced.

The men who ran Roosevelt Raceway, however, were convinced that Phillips was on the right track and gave him $40,000 in funds to develop the gate so that it could be used. It worked. In fact, it worked perfectly. It was given a test at Roosevelt in its 1946 meet, and it quickly wrought a revolution in starting races. Horsemen, even the old-timers, begrudgingly accepted it. Bettors appreciated the fair and reliable starts. And the Phillips gate spread throughout the sport like wildfire.

The combination of the starting gate and the end of World War II caused the harness meet at Roosevelt to explode. The betting figures from Roosevelt Raceway alone tell the tale vividly: In 1945, the average attendance was 9,743, and the betting averaged $240,951. The Long Island track celebrated its first $500,000 handle in the early summer of 1946. The following year, attendance jumped to an average of 14,189, and the average handle was $451,286. That record didn't last long. Handles in excess of $500,000 became routine, and two years later, in the summer of 1948, Roosevelt celebrated its first $1 million handle.

The income that Roosevelt realized from the betting and from parking, programs and concessions allowed it to offer ever-increasing bounties for the best horses in harness racing. In 1947, Doctor Spencer won the $25,000 American Trotting Championship, contested in two dashes at one mile. Two months later, April Star, who overcame a broken leg shortly after his birth, won the first Nassau Pace at Roosevelt. The two-mile event was contested for an astonishing purse of $40,000.

In 1949, Roosevelt raced 147 nights, and the attendance averaged more than fifteen thousand patrons per program. Betting averaged $648,144. (That is comparable to $6.1 million in 2012 dollars.) All bets, of course, were made on track through the parimutuel windows in that era.

Roosevelt's success did not go unnoticed. One person who was very familiar with the track's operations and bottom line was William H. Cane, the man who staged the Hambletonian at Good Time Park in Goshen. Cane

A History of Trotters, Tracks and Horsemen

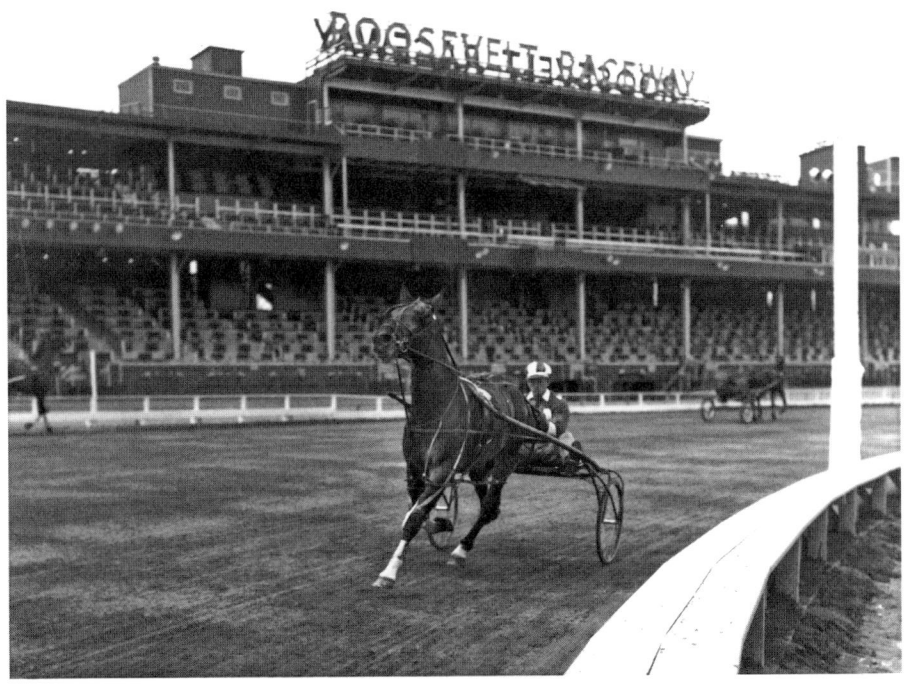

Horseman Billy Haughton takes his star pacer Carmel Boy into the first turn at the original Roosevelt Raceway, which was opened in 1940 and replaced by the "dream track" in 1957.

was an astute businessman, and he knew that New York City's metropolitan area was big enough to sustain two harness tracks. He cast his eyes on the old Empire City track in Yonkers that had been used as the site of the 1943 Hambletonian. The track was established in 1899 when William H. Clark built a one-mile track in Yonkers, but when Clark died the next year, the track stood vacant, tied up in litigation for seven years as Clark's heirs tried to sell it. It was intermittently used to host Thoroughbred racing.

It was virtually a turnkey operation when Cane purchased the property and got a license for a harness meet. Empire City was noted for its distinctive clubhouse in the track's first turn, an elegant if somewhat outdated structure. The new track would be called Yonkers Raceway to break with the old track's checkered past, and a new half-mile track with modern lighting replaced the old mile surface.

Opening night was a rousing success, to no one's surprise. When the first program was set to go on April 27, 1950, a crowd of 21,178 surged through the turnstiles and bet $688,009. The figures pleased everyone, and they were a hint of things to come. Like Roosevelt, its Long Island rival, Yonkers had no problem getting customers to come and bet the trotters. About 1 million people came to Yonkers to watch the seventy-three nights of racing in its inaugural 1950 season. That made for an average attendance of 14,766. The betting at the new track topped $50 million the first year for an average of $688,335.

Yonkers named its first signature event the Good Time Pace after Bill Cane's 1949 Little Brown Jug winner. It was contested over one and a half miles or three laps around the half-mile track, and the winner was the race's namesake. Good Time paced the distance in 3:08, and Bill Cane cashed the winner's check of the $25,000 purse.

The numbers only got better. By 1952, the attendance at Yonkers averaged over eighteen thousand, and the average handle was more than $1 million per night. The business was so brisk that Yonkers could offer munificent purses and make significant improvements in the physical plant. It pioneered double-deck barns that contained as many as seventy-eight stalls. For patrons, the innovative four-level Parkadrome parking structure made the most of the limited space that Yonkers had. The Empire Terrace dining room overlooked the track, and the Good Time Room, named for the great pacer, could accommodate six hundred racing fans.

The Good Time Pace continued to be a signature event at Yonkers during the 1950s as its purse jumped from $25,000 to $58,700 in 1960. The winners were Scottish Pence, Direct Rhythm, Wilmington's Star, Red Sails, Adios Harry, Diamond Hal, Duane Hanover, Speedy Pick and Bye Bye Byrd. Other events were started at Yonkers in an effort to showcase the best horses and to compete with the bounties offered at Roosevelt Raceway on Long Island.

It was an era of "full speed ahead" for harness racing.

The Fabulous '50s

New Tracks and New Races

In the fall of 1952, Americans agreed with the slogan "I Like Ike" and voted World War II military hero Dwight D. Eisenhower into the White House, replacing Harry Truman, who decided not to stand for election. After two decades of having a Democratic president—first Franklin D. Roosevelt and then Harry S Truman—voters opted to make a change. (In 1951, harness horse breeder Max Hempt was so anxious to bid adieu to Truman that he named a yearling colt Adios Harry in hopes the man from Missouri would leave office. Ironically, Adios Harry made history at New York tracks in the mid-1950s.)

As 1953 dawned, the Empire State had prosperous parimutuel plants at Roosevelt and Yonkers in the metropolitan area, as well as Batavia and Buffalo in the western reaches of the state. Upstate, the action was focused on Saratoga Raceway. What was clearly missing was a track in the heart of it all to provide opportunities for mid-state racing fans to witness the burgeoning business of harness racing and to give horsemen from that region a chance to showcase their stock. But plans were afoot to fill that need.

In the late 1940s, an attorney from Oneida, New York, named William B. Kelley visited Saratoga's harness plant and liked what he saw. He liked it so much, in fact, that he thought his part of the state should have something just like it. The Hambletonian's brief stand at Syracuse was almost two decades in the rearview mirror, and the only races were at the fairs. Kelley was advised to speak to New Yorker Clarence F. Gaines, a longtime devotee of the sulky sport who operated the resplendent Gainesway Farm in the Bluegrass. Gaines and Kelley later brought in Octave Blake, then president

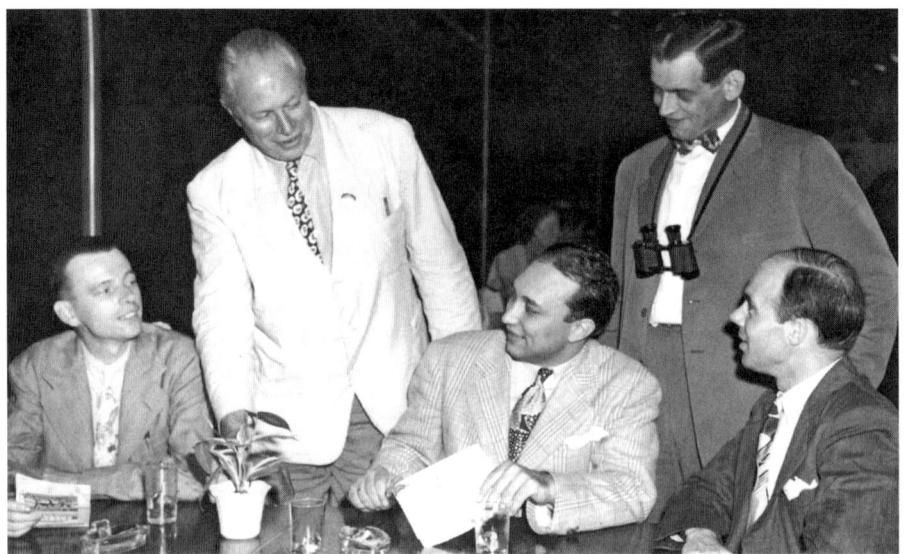

Two Upstate lawyers prominent in the establishment of Saratoga Raceway were Frank Wiswall (standing left) and Ernest Morris (standing right). They're shown here in the Saratoga clubhouse discussing business.

of the Grand Circuit. The push for a parimutuel track in central New York was gaining steam.

Veteran racing official Ed Keller was hired as the general manager of the would-be track, and the owners quietly snapped up some farmland near Collamer, east of Syracuse. Soon, however, they met with violent opposition from local religious groups, and they decided to switch instead of fighting. Some central New York horsemen hoped to establish a track in the small town of Vernon, which already had a fairground. The investors bought the 80-acre fairground and 260 adjoining acres. They now had what they thought was an ideal site.

Gaines, Blake and Keller had been in harness racing for many years and revered its traditions, but when they broke ground for the new track in Vernon, they also broke with tradition in the size of the track. Historically, one-mile tracks had been the classic size for harness races, but to bring the action close to the fans, half-mile tracks became all the rage in the post–World War II era. Then they learned about a track near Detroit called Hazel Park that was five-eighths of a mile in circumference. It seemed to offer all the benefits of having the action close to the public while avoiding the tight turns and short stretches of a half-mile track.

A History of Trotters, Tracks and Horsemen

The Vernon group, however, decided to bump up the circumference of the track a furlong to three-quarters of a mile and have the races start from an extended chute that connected to the top of the homestretch. This revolutionary design seemed to offer benefits to everyone. It would certainly be safer for drivers, as the horses would travel more than a quarter-mile before reaching the first turn. It would eliminate many of the obvious post position biases found at tracks. And having two turns to the mile instead of three would allow for faster times in the speed-crazed sport of harness racing. From the bettors' perspective, it would allow for racing to go more to form. The best horse would win more often because luck would be less of a factor in the races.

The new track, Vernon Downs, halfway between Syracuse and Utica, opened on July 1, 1953. The public found a brilliantly illuminated oval; the twenty-six light poles positioned around the track gave off more than 1.2 million watts of electricity. The grandstand area and parking lot (accommodating five thousand cars) were also brightly lit for customers. "There probably is no track in the country that has a better illuminated grandstand area," said an article in *Hoof Beats* magazine.

Twenty-four barns, each with twenty-four stalls, provided ample accommodations for the horses at the initial meet. The stable area included six blacksmith shops, a harness shop and a track kitchen—all the amenities a horseman could ever want. The paddock had eighty-eight stalls. Best of all, perhaps, was the natural setting of the new track, as spectators could look across the track to a vista of verdant foothills.

Despite the best efforts of the track officials, some of the finishing touches at Vernon Downs were left incomplete on opening night. Labor strikes hampered the flow of last-minute activity. Track president Octave Blake used the public address system to explain the difficulties to an understanding first-night crowd.

The first race on July 1 was contested at 6.5 furlongs and went to Bob Abbe II, a son of Bert Abbe. He paid a hefty $38.60 for a $2.00 winning bet. The featured $2,000.00 trot went to Syndicator, a black son of Spencer Scott, driven by Garland Garnsey, a veteran New York horseman. (His son, Glen, would one day be a top driver himself at Vernon Downs and earn admission into the Hall of Fame three decades later.)

A few weeks after the opening, Hi-Lo's Forbes, the top pacer then in training, made a stop at Vernon Downs and came away with a gate-to-wire win in 1:59, a new track mark for the new track. He came back a week later and equaled that mark. Hi-Lo's Forbes was just getting started, as a week later he notched a 1:58 mile at Vernon. This was speed seldom seen at parimutuel tracks in the 1950s.

In other events at Vernon in late July 1953, two sophomore trotters were turning in impressive miles. Kimberly Kid won for driver Tom Berry, and the filly Helicopter triumphed for driver Jimmy Arthur, an assistant in the Delvin Miller stable. A few weeks later, Helicopter and Kimberly Kid met in the Hambletonian at Good Time Park in Goshen, and the filly prevailed over the colt in a three-heat battle.

The principals at Vernon Downs were interested in presenting more than just ordinary races for ordinary horses. They wanted to showcase the best in harness racing. From that inaugural season, Vernon laid out a schedule of stakes races that would elevate it to status as one of the top-flight tracks in the expanding Standardbred galaxy.

At a time when most harness tracks were half-milers, Vernon Down was the largest raceway in circumference east of the Mississippi. There were several mile tracks at state fairs (in addition to the famed Red Mile in Kentucky), but Vernon was the largest track with an extended parimutuel meet. That meant it recorded far more 2:00 miles in that era than most tracks. Time has always been important in the sport, and in the 1950s, a 2:00 mile was still considered a "miracle mile" or "magic mile." The list of trotters and pacers with 2:00 records was often call the "charmed list."

In the summer of 1958, just before America celebrated its birthday on the Fourth of July, the seventh parimutuel harness track in New York opened just north of the small town of Monticello in Sullivan County. At first, it might have seemed to be a strange location for a racetrack. Monticello had about five thousand residents, and the new track was ninety miles northwest of New York City. Where would the new track find its customers? The founders of the track knew that there was gold in the nearby Catskills Mountains: thousands of summer vacationers. The area had long been a getaway haven for city dwellers, and Monticello was initially deemed to be a "resort track." After all, there were 385 hotels with eighty-five thousand guests and sixteen thousand employees in that track's market area.

Those statistics motivated Franklin Devlin, who had served on the board of directors at Roosevelt Raceway, to seize the moment. He joined forces with local businessmen to form the Sullivan Country Harness Racing Association to make the $5 million investment to develop the new track. Devlin knew from his experience at Roosevelt just how profitable a harness track could be. The investors found a 246-acre site that had superb highway access and that sat in a natural bowl. Two tracks, both a half-mile in circumference, were

A History of Trotters, Tracks and Horsemen

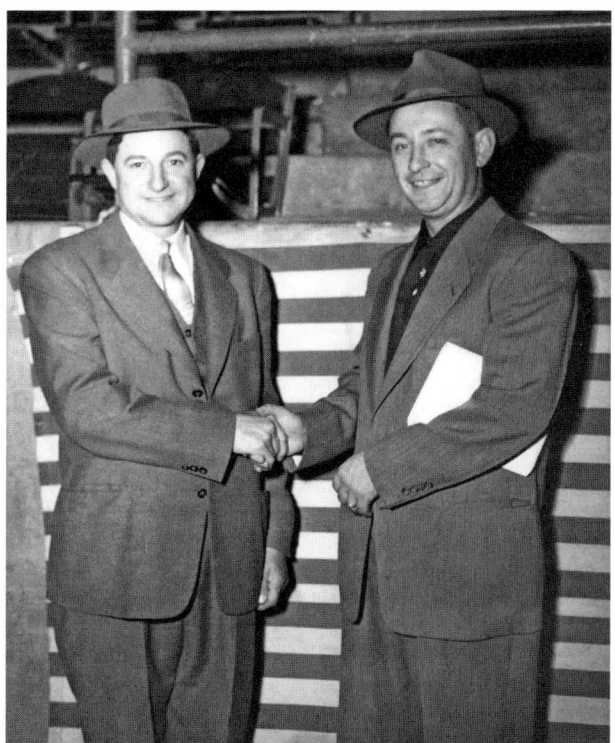

Two great horsemen with significant impact on New York racing during its postwar boom years. On the left is Levi Harner, who trained for New York owner Ted Zornow. He's shaking hands with Billy Haughton, harness racing's perpetual motion man, whose stable dominated the racing at Roosevelt and Yonkers for decades.

constructed. One was for training and the other for racing. The investors took pride in the state-of-the-art lighting system to be used at the new track. The combination grandstand and clubhouse could accommodate four thousand customers.

Twenty concrete block barns, each with thirty stalls, were built, and the prevailing joke around the track was that the stalls were so roomy they could easily be converted into motel rooms if the track was not successful. Monticello was only thirty miles up the road from Goshen, the Cradle of the Trotter, but the area was known for its resort hotels and nightclubs instead of trotters.

Devlin knew that getting good horses to Monticello would require some enticement, so Monticello participated in the Trans-America Series to lure some of the biggest names in the sulky sport to the new track. He hired Chares Larkin as his director of racing, and young James J. Dunnigan Jr. would be his assistant.

On opening night, June 27, 1958, some 6,369 people came to see what the new track had to offer. Patrons ponied up $246,893 in bets that night. Officials were gratified with the turnout but acknowledged that the real

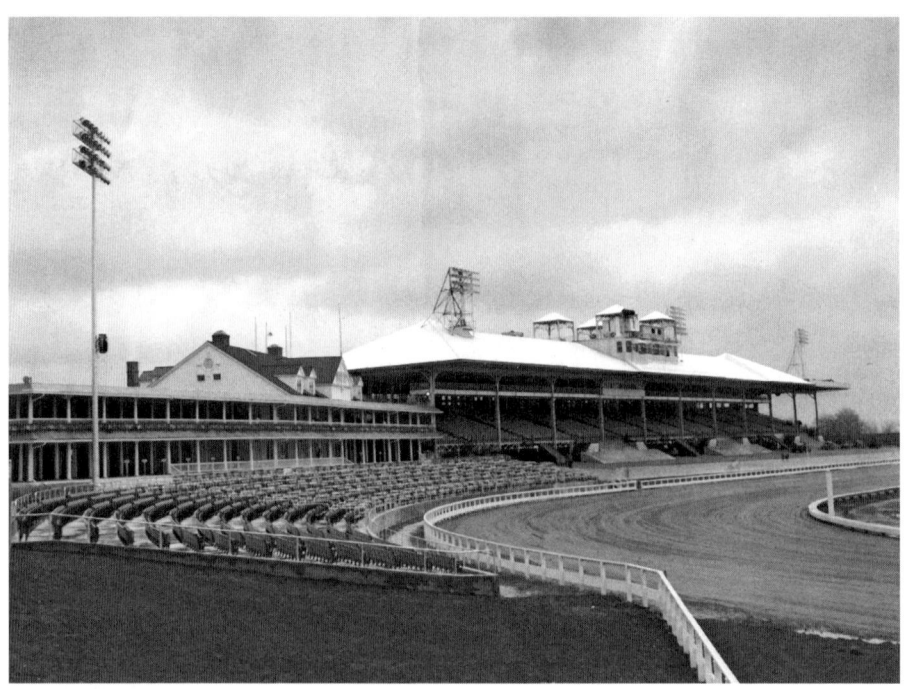

Yonkers Raceway, established in 1950 on the site of the old Empire City track, retained the old track's distinctive clubhouse on the first turn.

vacation season in the Catskills started after Independence Day. They expected even larger crowds then. The opening night feature was a $7,500 C Pace that featured the cat-quick free-legged filly Good Counsel, a world champion as a two-year-old, among the entries. Alas, she cut a leg warming up and had to be scratched. The race went to Canny Scot, a five-year-old son of Scottish Pence in 2:04.3. Future Hall of Famer Vernon Dancer drove the winner. New York lieutenant governor George B. Deluca and New York Harness Racing commissioner George P. Monahan presented the trophy.

In mid-August, some of the best pacers in the nation came to Monticello for the Trans-America Series, sponsored by Harness Tracks of America. The select field of six was composed of Speedy Pick, Widower Creed, Robert Lee Frost, Grand H. Volo, Pegarno and the mare Belle Acton. The result was "ladies first" as Belle Acton and driver Billy Haughton showed the way to the wire in a new track record of 2:00.2. Speedy Pick and driver Charlie Fitzpatrick set the fractions and clung to the lead as the field turned into the stretch but had little to offer when Belle Acton launched her bid. She won by a half length over Speedy Pick. Widower Creed was a close third. The

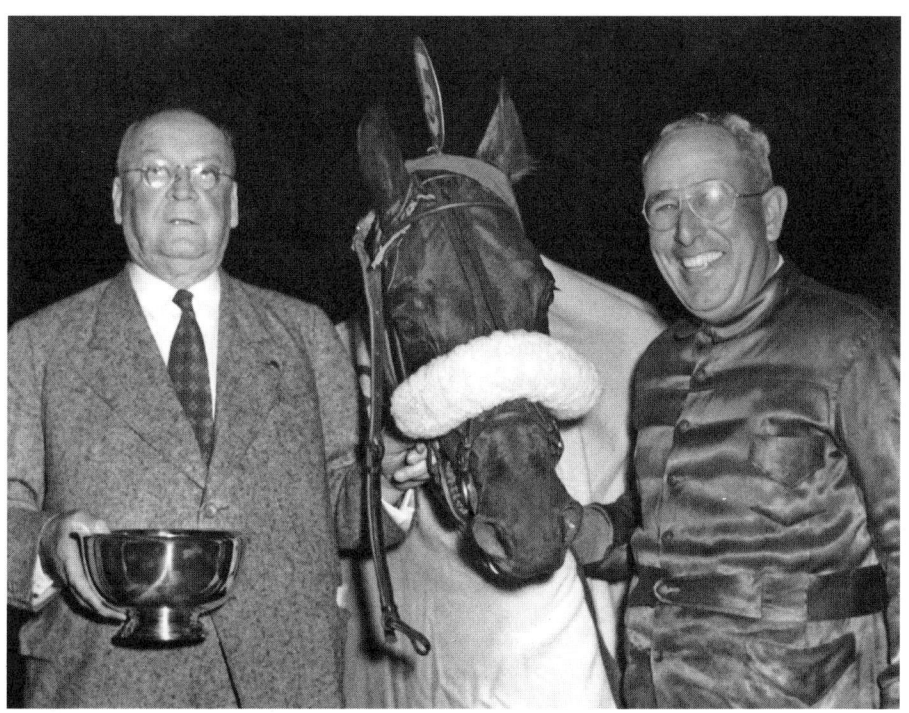

Few horses enjoyed more popularity in the postwar boom than Good Time, a pint-sized pacer with a huge will to win. He's shown here with owner-breeder William H. Cane and trainer-driver Frank Ervin.

victory made Belle Acton the richest Standardbred mare in history and gave her thirteen wins in fifteen starts in the 1958 season.

When the inaugural season at Monticello ended in late September, a total of $12.4 million had been bet by the 326,623 people who attended. Track officials pointed out that rainy weather affected business many nights, but they were pleased with the financial outcome and looked forward to the 1959 season.

In the mid-1950s it became apparent that the Hambletonian would leave the Empire State for a location in southern Illinois. The loss of such a prestigious race was softened by the start of new races at the metropolitan half-mile tracks.

In 1955, Yonkers Raceway launched two sophomore events: the Yonkers Futurity for trotters and the William H. Cane Futurity for pacers. They carried purses that made them irresistible to horsemen and owners. The Yonkers Futurity paid out $73,840 in 1955, almost as much as the $86,863 offered in the Hambletonian. The Cane Pace carried a purse of $71,040, higher than the $66,608 offered to the starters in the Little Brown Jug. Quick Chief with New York native Billy Haughton in the sulky won the Cane Pace, while the Yonkers Futurity was taken by Scott Frost.

Not to be outdone, Roosevelt Raceway decided to offer its own jackpot purse for sophomore pacers starting in 1956. It created the Messenger Stakes, named after the stallion responsible for founding the breed. Its first edition carried a purse of $71,500, almost $20,000 more than the lucre offered in the 1956 Little Brown Jug. These new races upset the traditions of racing. Heretofore, horsemen had always pointed their top three-year-old trotters to the Hambletonian and the Kentucky Futurity in Lexington. These were classics that every trainer and owner wanted to win. With pacers, the biggest prize was the Little Brown Jug. But how could anyone afford to ignore the jackpots offered by the tracks in the Big Apple?

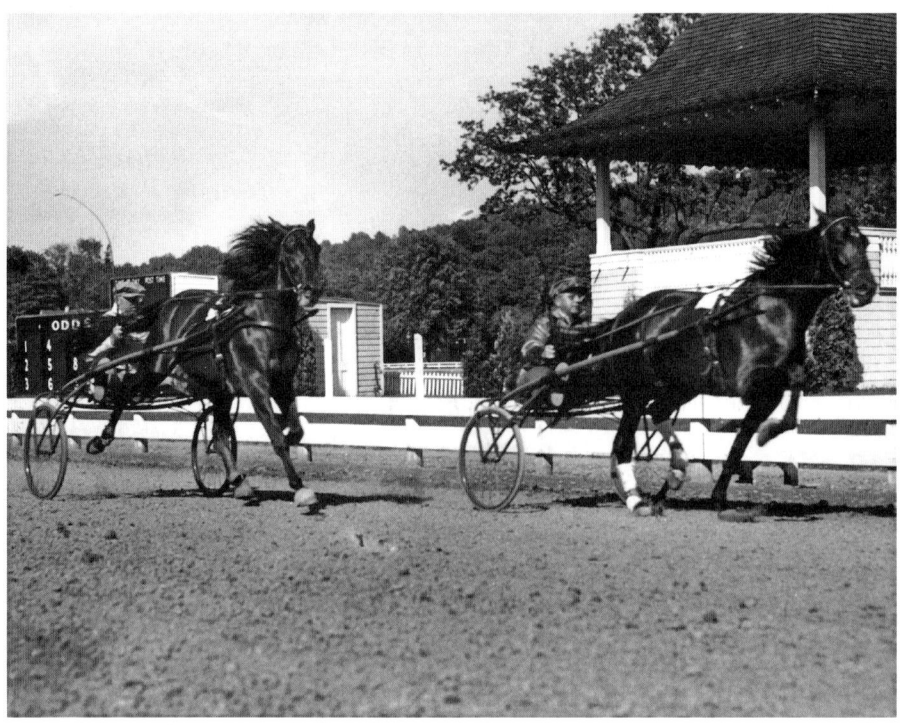

Florican (inside) with Harry Pownall and Star's Pride with Joe McFadden were raced by Harriman and the Arden Homestead Stable. They're shown in a training mile at Historic Track. Both trotters later became influential stallions.

A History of Trotters, Tracks and Horsemen

Simply put, they couldn't. Everyone took notice of the rich races at Yonkers and Roosevelt and adjusted their racing schedules accordingly to accommodate those race dates. Leaders in harness racing seized on these new races to create trotting and pacing counterparts of the famed Triple Crown for Thoroughbreds. It was deemed that the Triple Crown for trotters would consist of the Hambletonian, Kentucky Futurity and the Yonkers Futurity. The pacing version would include the Little Brown Jug, Messenger and Cane Futurity. That put half of harness racing's six Triple Crown events at New York tracks: the Messenger, Cane and Yonkers Futurity.

The purses for the new races at the two tracks started high and simply kept growing. The Messenger became the first $100,000 pacing event in harness history in its second year in 1957—it was won by Delvin Miller driving Meadow Lands. By 1961, it was raced for $145,377. That year, it was won by Adios Don. Roosevelt Raceway was then the best track in harness racing, and it didn't like to play second fiddle to its crosstown rival in purses. The Yonkers Trot had started at $73,840 but jumped to $100,330 when Duke Rodney won it in 1961; the Cane Pace went from $71,040 in its first year to $110,950 by 1961, when Cold Front was the winner.

The first Messenger Stakes in 1956 was won by Billy Haughton and the fabulous filly Belle Acton. She went on to become a redoubtable mare even as she matured, and she seldom had problems in putting away her male counterparts. Most pacing fillies are not competitive with males, but Belle Acton was an exception. Another was Countess Adios, a graceful bay filly that raced "free-legged," or without the help of hobbles to maintain her gait. She beat the best colts of her class in both the Cane Pace and Messenger in 1960. Countess Adios might well have become the first female ever to win the Little Brown Jug, but she was not eligible for that classic in central Ohio. In the half-century after Countess Adios took the Messenger, no female won the Messenger Stakes. (The Little Brown Jug had started in 1946, and the first filly to win it was Fan Hanover in 1981. She will likely continue to hold that unique status because no filly was even started in the Jug in the next thirty years.)

In the mid-1950s, New York businessman Marty Tananbaum, along with brothers Al and Stanley, took over ownership of Yonkers Raceway from founder William H. Cane. Attendance for the 85-night meet was about 1.6 million, and total handle was at $100.0 million. The Tananbaums went to work, and soon nights with more than $2.0 million in handle became far more frequent. In the 105-night meet in 1956, the total attendance jumped

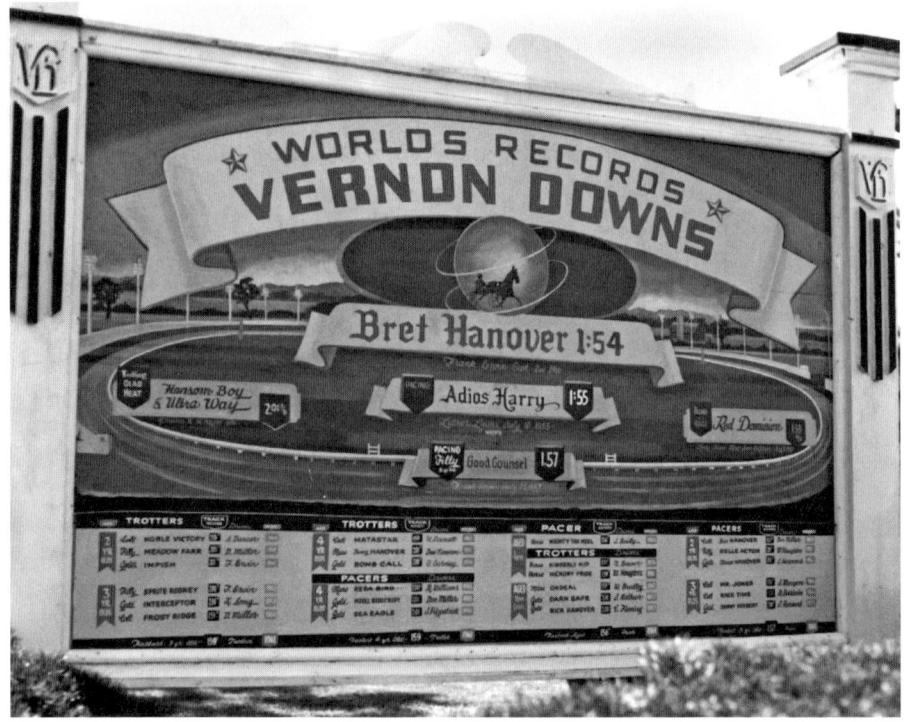

Vernon Downs was justifiably proud of the many fast miles over its innovative three-fourths-mile oval, and the record board at the track was the track's way of saluting its many record holders.

to more than 2.0 million, and the handle jumped to $140.4 million. The numbers continued to climb. In 1957, attendance was 2.1 million, and the handle inched up to $145.6 million.

The Tananbaums were raised in the Bronx by immigrant parents who operated a textile business. The brothers operated the business after their father died, and it was Marty who took the most active role when they acquired Yonkers. Marty was a mover and shaker in breeding circles as he established White Devon Farm in Geneseo and later took an active role in establishing the New York Sire Stakes.

Yonkers was known then as the "Giant of Trotting," but Marty Tananbaum also made the track a giant in the community through his tireless charitable and civic work. He raised millions of dollars for the City of Hope and children with special needs and was also committed to the Jewish Theological Seminary, New York Mirror Welfare Fund and the Young Men's Philanthropic League, among his many activities.

A History of Trotters, Tracks and Horsemen

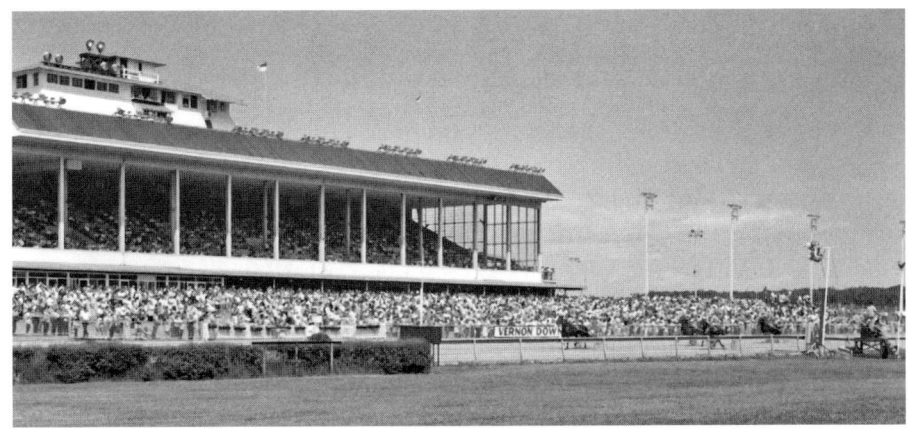

Vernon Downs in central New York introduced a unique three-fourths-mile racing oval when it opened in 1953, and it gained a reputation as a place where trainers could develop their stakes prospects. It also hosted many world-record miles.

Tananbaum was a firm proponent of stakes for young horses and implemented many lucrative stakes at Yonkers. He considered the New York Sire Stakes (NYSS) to be his brainchild, and the first NYSS events were contested at Yonkers. Other tracks were enjoying prosperity, too. In 1957, Batavia Downs launched a modernization program that would stretch over a decade and culminate with the expansion and enclosure of the grandstand. Before enclosing the grandstand, patrons were warmed by an infrared radiant heating system.

Harness racing took significant steps forward off the track, too, during the 1950s. In the Goshen, a museum was established to collect memorabilia and to honor the greats—both human and equine—in the sport. The museum was located in what had once been the home of Bill Cane's famed Good Time Stable, a racing powerhouse that included some of the biggest names in the sport. The lovely old Tudor building on Main Street in Goshen was the perfect setting for a museum since it was adjacent to Historic Track.

The founders of the museum put forth the money to acquire the building and transform it from a stable to a showcase for harness racing history. They prevailed on owners and trainers to donate items of historic significance to the new museum to seed the exhibits and thus create interest for racing fans.

In 1953, the trustees of the Harness Racing Museum decided to honor the pioneers in harness racing by creating an Immortals section of the pantheon. First they recognized the greatest four-legged stars in the sport, starting, of course, with Hambletonian himself, the Big Daddy of harness racing. Peter the Great was also in that first class, as were many other stellar trotters and pacers.

A few years later, the museum began to highlight the people who had contributed so much to the early years of the sport. Among the first honorees were W.J. Andrews, Charles Backman, C.K.G. Billings, William H. Cane, Will Caton, Walter Cox, H.K. Devereux, John H. Dickerson, Budd Doble, John L. Dodge, Harry Fleming, Vic Fleming, J. Malcoln Forbes, Edward F. "Pop" Geers, C.J. Hamlin, Lamon V. Harkness, Frank C. Jones, David Look, Gus Macey, John E. Madden, Charles Marvin, W.H. McCarthy, Michael McDevitt, Myron McHenry, Richard McMahon, Septer Palin, Walter Palmer, H.M. Parshall, C.W. Phellis, W.N. Reynolds, William Rysdyk, Joseph Serrill, John Splan, Leland Stanford, Ben White, Charles Williams and Hiram Woodruff.

The museum started modestly, but it became an important part of the enduring appeal of the Cradle of the Trotter in the heart of Orange County. When trotting devotees flocked to Goshen for the racing at Good Time Park or Historic Track, a stop at the museum was always part of the itinerary.

People active in harness racing in that era believed that the sport had a future that seemed unlimited, but tradition has always important, too, and honoring the stars of the past gained increasing importance as support for the museum grew. It was fitting that the museum was located in Goshen because the Empire State, to paraphrase Shakespeare, bestrode the harness racing world in the 1950s and '60s like a colossus.

Harness Racing's Mecca

On the first day of August 1957, a new era in racing dawned at Roosevelt Raceway. The new $19 million facility was immediately dubbed the "dream track" by everyone. People stood slack-jawed in amazement at its amenities. For George Morton Levy, it was simply a dream come true.

More than anything else, the "new" Roosevelt Raceway was a validation that harness racing had indeed arrived in the major leagues of American sports. Many bettors had first seen the trotting and pacing sport on the dusty tracks at county fairgrounds, but those days seemed like dim memories under the glare of the bright lights on Long Island.

Certainly there was nothing comparable even in the elite levels of the Thoroughbred world. Fans were amazed that they could follow the races on large screens in the grandstand and clubhouse. Even the ink-stained wretches in the press box had their own closed-circuit television feed. No one missed the calls of the track announcer because Roosevelt had 1,200 loudspeakers as part of what was called the largest low-volume public address system ever installed. Roosevelt could afford these wonders because betting had boomed from $28.5 million in 1945 to $126.5 million a decade later.

Levy knew from his experience in the early years at Roosevelt that the track's take of the betting revenue was only one source of income. There was also parking and programs. One of the Levy legends that survives is that he occasionally wore a lapel pin depicting a hot dog. When asked the raison d'être for this seeming bit of whimsy, Levy said that he made a lot of money selling hot dogs to the bettors at the track.

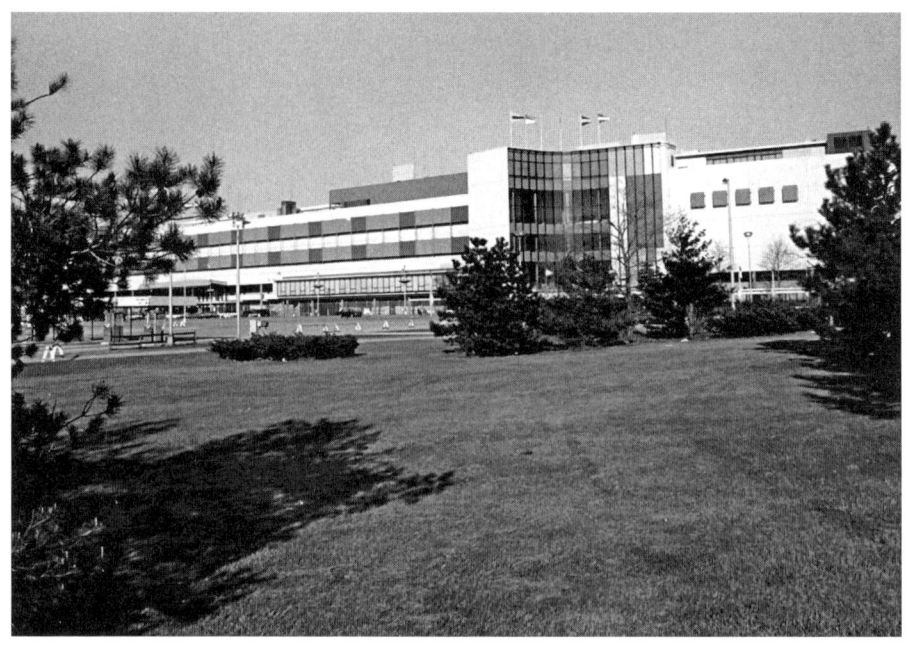

Harness racing's "dream track" was the new Roosevelt Raceway, which replaced the historic structure. The steel and glass facility boasted every modern convenience for customers and horsemen.

By the late 1950s, Roosevelt was clearly the dominant track in North America. It offered the biggest races, attracted the best horses, boasted the best colony of horsemen and commanded the loyalty of thousands of racing fans spread across the sprawling New York metropolitan area. It's said that Alexander the Great wept when he had no more worlds to conquer, but George Morton Levy and his associates at Roosevelt entertained no such notions. Besides, while they had indeed conquered North America, there was still a world of trotting unknown to American racing fans.

That was the genesis of the Roosevelt International, a trotting magnet designed to lure the best trotters from around the world to the half-mile oval on Long Island. It wasn't an easy task, nor was it inexpensive. Management realized that it would have to pick up the travel costs for the horses and people coming from Europe. Roosevelt sent teams to various European nations to see which trotters were the best available and to see if they could lure them to a new race in America.

One stumbling block was that European horses were accustomed to performing over much longer distances than the one-mile standard

A History of Trotters, Tracks and Horsemen

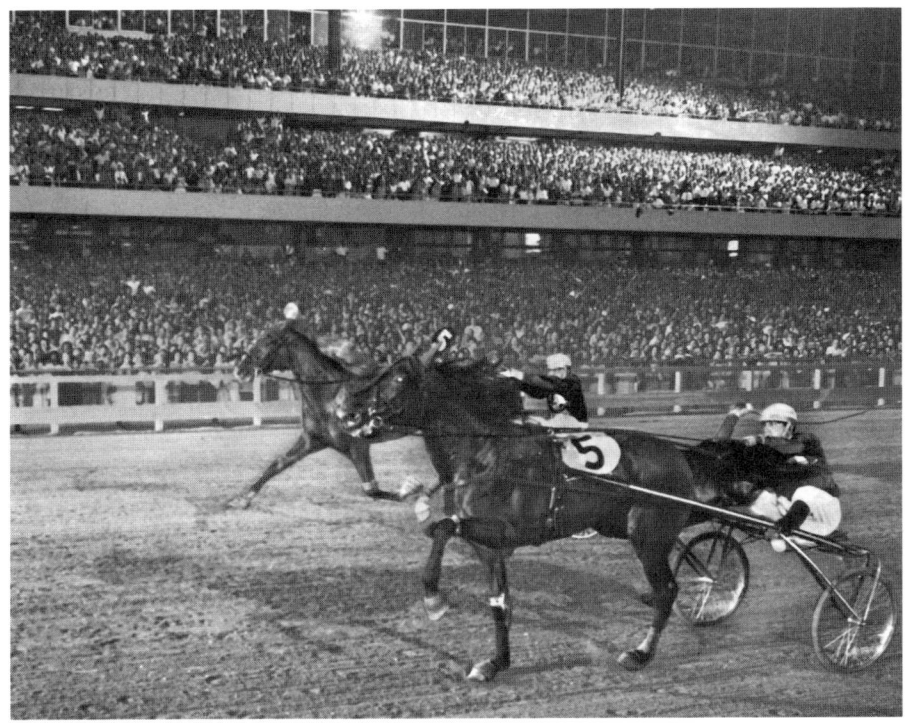

Jamin of France wins the first International Trot at Roosevelt Raceway in 1959, an event that brought unprecedented media attention to harness racing.

customary in North America. Another concern was that Roosevelt was a half-mile track, much smaller than the spacious tracks in Europe. How would the invaders do getting around the tights turns of the Roosevelt track? Nothing could be done, of course, to change the circumference of the track, but Roosevelt agreed to contest the International Trot as a distance of one and a half miles to make it more appealing to the European marathoners.

To sweeten the pot for foreign horses, Roosevelt offered a $50,000 purse, a bonanza too irresistible for the European trotters to resist. An invitation to the Roosevelt International carried enormous prestige, plus the chance for a trotter's connections to come to New York to sightsee and enjoy the races as the guests of Roosevelt Raceway.

The enticements were more than enough. A half dozen horses traveled to New York in the summer of 1959 to challenge the American representative, Trader Horn, and the Canadian champ Philip Frost. From Norway came Jens Protector; Tornese and Icare IV came from Italy; the German

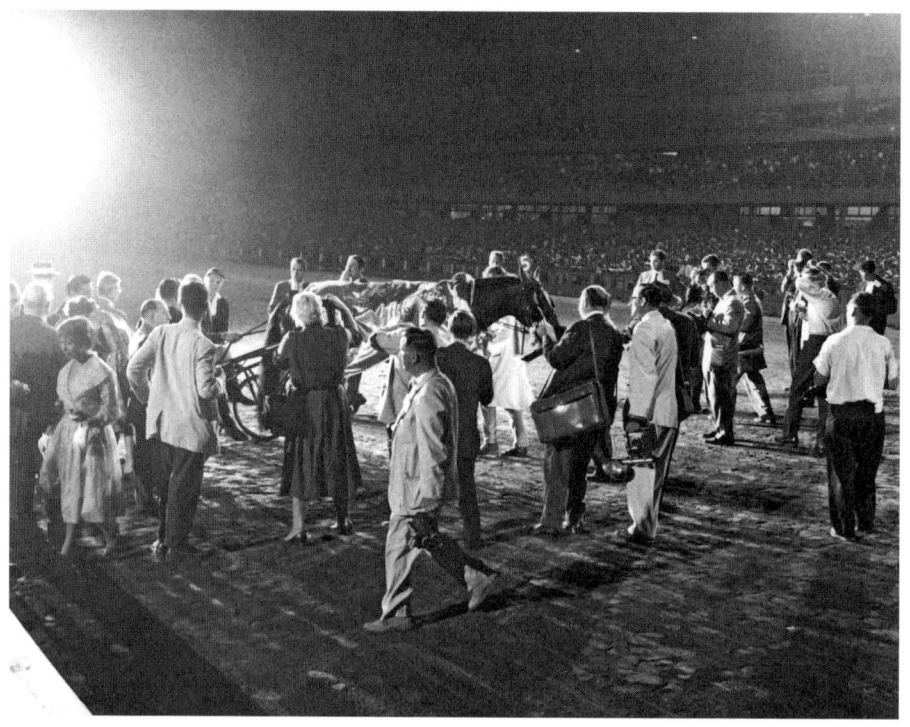

The post-race fanfare after Jamin's win was all part of the spectacular show that Roosevelt's public relations director Nick Grande orchestrated.

representative was Ivacourt; Jamin carried the tricolor of France; and Adept was shipped from New Zealand.

The New York daily newspapers lavished attention on the event, and Roosevelt's publicity director, Nick Grande, made certain that they had plenty to write about. The French star, Jamin, enjoyed a diet that included artichokes, and the Roosevelt publicity team milked that novel angle for all it was worth.

Bettors from the Big Apple weren't certain that the invaders were worthy challengers for the local boys. In fact, the Roosevelt regular Trader Horn with his driver Billy Haughton was deemed to be such a likely winner that his post-time odds dropped below even money. Tornese of Italy was the second choice at 4-1. Those Americans more familiar with European racing, however, knew that Jamin of France and driver Jean Riaud should not be discounted. Norman Woolworth, a young owner living in New York but familiar with the French classics, nicknamed Jamin "Creeping Death" for

A History of Trotters, Tracks and Horsemen

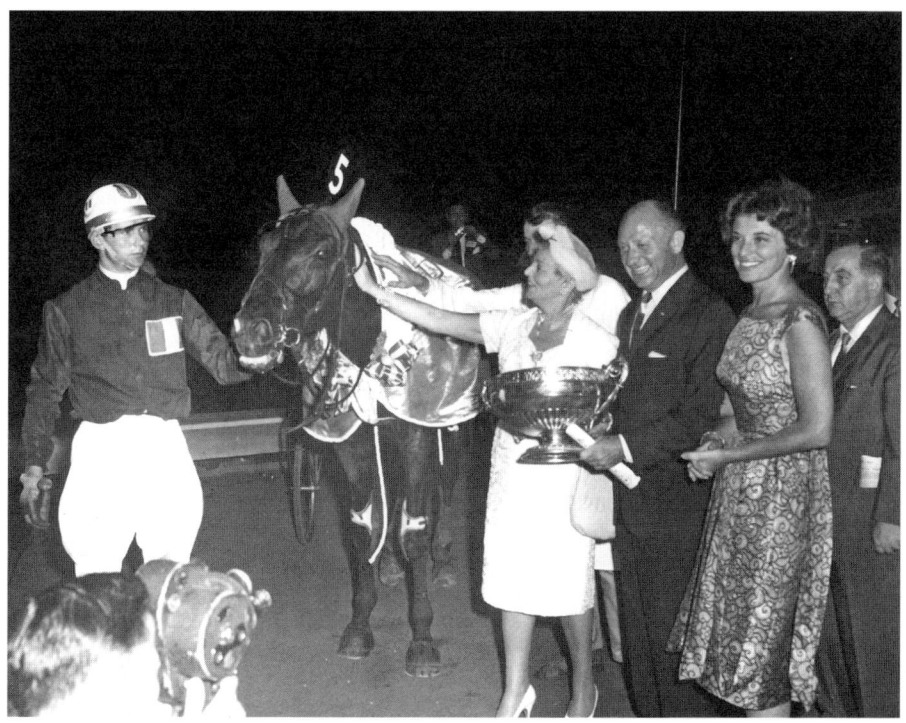

Trainer-driver Jean Riaud stands proudly with Jamin, while Madame Olry-Roederer, Jamin's owner, stands at the right. She was so nervous prior to the race that she couldn't watch it.

his relentless pursuit of any horse in front of him. The French trotters, Woolworth knew, simply didn't know when to quit.

On the day of the race, fans showed up at Roosevelt well in advance of 6:00 p.m., when the gates were opened. In fact, by 4:00 p.m. the parking lot was halfway full. By post time, more than forty-eight thousand patrons had jammed every corner of the spacious grandstand. When the international combatants entered the track, the lights went out at Roosevelt, and each horse was introduced to the crowd illuminated by a rooftop spotlight. The horses were saluted with music from their native land.

As starter Steve Phillips sent the trotters away, Jens Protector broke stride and Tornese took the lead. He was challenged on the outside by the bold Canadian Philip Frost, who took control. Jamin was back in the pack, having lost his gait when he encountered the sharp first turn.

Early in the race, the favorite Trader Horn was in high gear, and the crowd roared as he took control. Then Philip Frost also broke stride. It seemed to be Trader Horn's race. Then Trader Horn's driver, Billy Haughton, looked over his right shoulder and saw Creeping Death coming at him. And coming. And coming. Trader Horn faltered. Jamin didn't. Jamin surged to the front in the stretch, while Tornese passed the tiring Trader Horn.

Jamin's victory touched off an enormous celebration as the French connections poured onto the track and greeted the trotting hero with jubilation. Madame Leon Olry-Roederer, Jamin's owner, had been so nervous that she couldn't bear to watch the race and listened to the call from the dressing room of the track directors' lounge. Fireworks exploded in the sky over Roosevelt to herald the winner. And praise flowed for the track and for Jamin.

"I said this Jamin could take anything we've got," said famed horseman Delvin Miller. "I saw him over there [France] and, I want to tell you, this is a race horse. The guys over here just wouldn't believe me. Maybe they'll listen now." J. Alfred Valentine, the executive vice-president of Roosevelt, said, "This will lift the prestige of our sport immeasurably." His colleague Alvin Weil added, "I hope this will produce a great interchange of trotters between

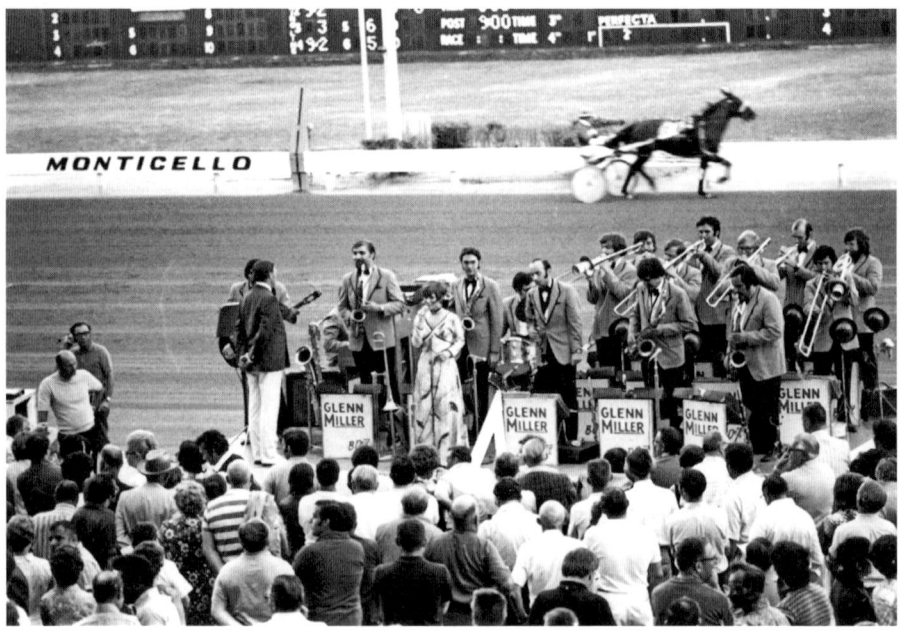

Monticello Raceway was always an innovator in bringing entertainment to its racing fans. The half-mile track in the Catskills featured many zany promotions over the years, but the track made sure that its patrons were entertained and had a memorable time when they went to the races.

A History of Trotters, Tracks and Horsemen

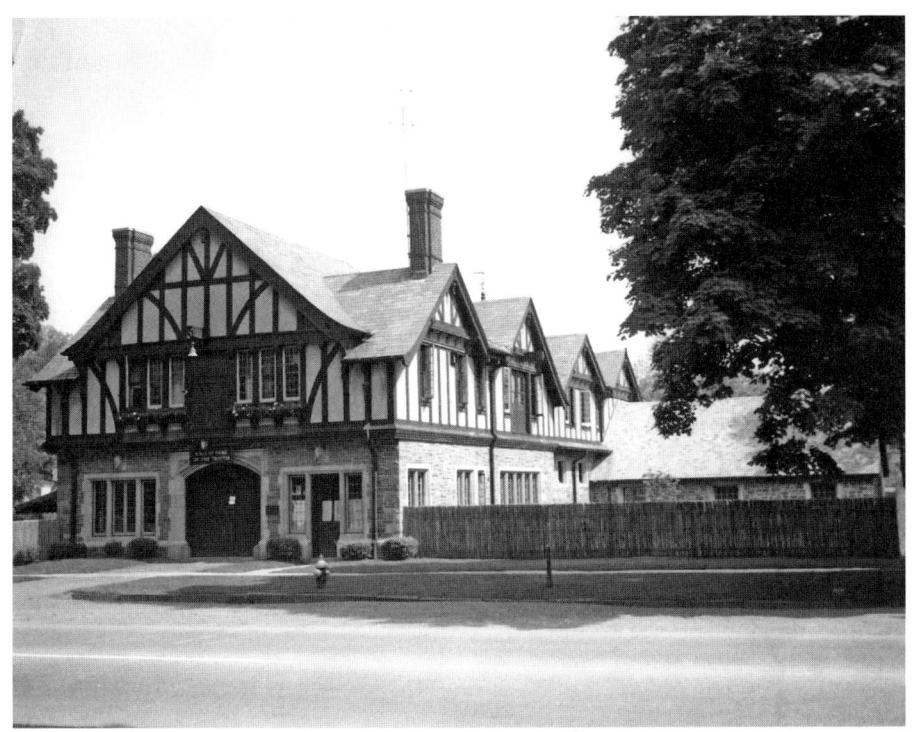

This classic Tudor structure on Main Street in Goshen was the base for William H. Cane's Good Time Stable for many years. Then it was converted into the Harness Racing Museum.

us and the continent." George Morton Levy summed it up by saying, "All the work, all the pains—it was worth it."

Jamin may have conquered his rivals, but Roosevelt Raceway had conquered the world of trotting. Throughout Europe, the Roosevelt International became known simply as the "world championship," and it was the dream of everyone on the continent with a decent trotter.

The second Roosevelt International was shortened to one and a quarter miles, and once again bettors picked the local American boys, Silver Song and driver Howard Camden, as the post time favorite. Silver Song was coming off a win over Steamin' Demon and Tyson Scott in the American Trotting Championship the previous week.

Racing fans remembered what a great show Roosevelt had put on for the first International and made sure they didn't miss the sequel. The largest crowd ever at a parimutuel harness raceway, 54,861, flocked to Roosevelt. "There never was a night like this at any harness track in the world," wrote journalist Leonard Lewin. "The excitement generated by this international competition for trotters inundated the fans, who created a historic crush that nearly exhausted the resourcefulness of track management." Lewin compared the atmosphere to the World Series, a major prize fight or "Sinatra at the Copa." "In a sense," he wrote, "this was Broadway come to Westbury. The people like the color of the race: the way it is staged from start to finish. It's a thrilling thing to see the lights go out and, as the trotters walk slowly down the track in front of the jammed stands under a following spotlight, you hear music indigenous to each country which has been carefully and cleverly selected and put on tape for the pre-race show."

In the race, Silver Song had the rail and made the most of it, seizing the lead early before yielding to Icare IV, competing in his second straight Roosevelt International. Parked outside of the leader was the 5-1 shot Hairos II of Holland, toting driver Wim Geersen, who weighed almost three hundred pounds. While the overland journey with the heavy load would tire most trotters, the French-bred Hairos II was impervious to the extra distance and extra load and rallied in the stretch to win.

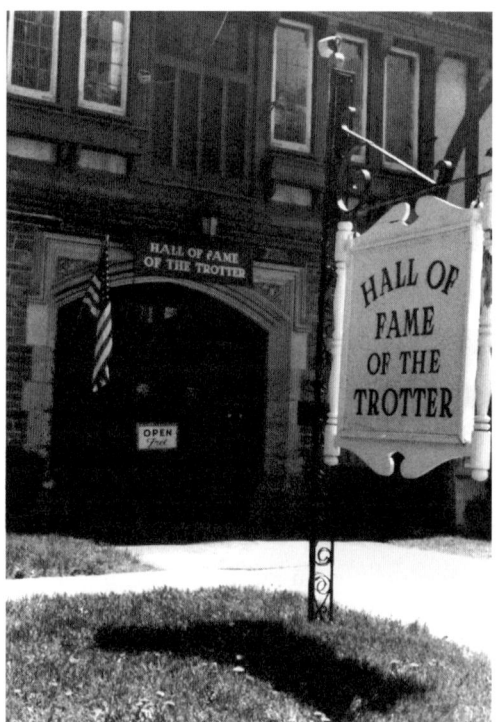

The Hall of Fame of the Trotter at the museum was a popular stop for horsemen and owners when Grand Circuit racing was held each summer in Goshen.

While Roosevelt was establishing its international classic, Yonkers was watching carefully. It couldn't very well host another international trotting event, so instead it decided to establish its own International Pace. The participants would be drawn from North America and Australia and New Zealand, as pacers were forbidden on the continent of Europe.

Yonkers took a different approach with its International Pace and inaugurated it in 1960 as a three-race series of varying distances: one mile, one and a

A History of Trotters, Tracks and Horsemen

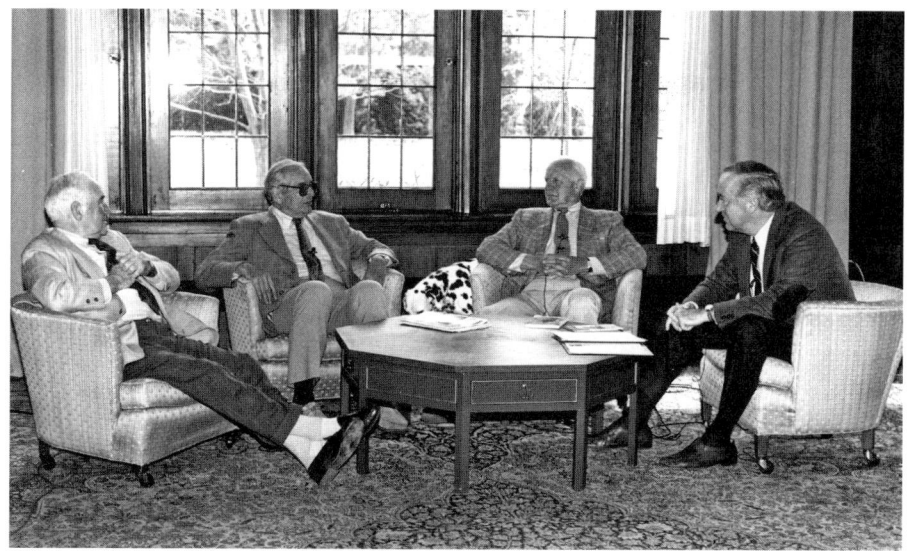

Three men of monumental importance to New York harness racing sit with Phil Pines (right), director of the Harness Racing Museum for an interview. *From left to right*: Elbridge Gerry Sr., Ernest Morris and Dunbar Bostwick. Pine recorded their memories in a series of "Cracker Barrel" interviews. *Author's collection.*

quarter miles and one and a half miles. Each leg carried a purse of $50,000. It was slated to get underway in the spring.

The one-and-a-quarter-mile leg of the race went to Bye Bye Byrd and Clint Hodgins, while the marathon twelve-furlong leg was taken by Widower Creed, driven by Howard Beissinger. The final leg, the one-mile race, came down to a heart-stopping duel between Champ Volo of Canada and Caduceus of New Zealand. The two pacers hit the wire together in 2:01.1, and the judges called for a photo finish print to see if they could separate them at the wire. The photo told the tale: it was a dead heat. The judges, however, weren't happy with the drive of Jack Litten behind Caduceus and disqualified him, placing Caduceus fourth.

The following year, the series was reduced to a single one-and-a-half-mile event contested for $50,000. A field of seven sidewheelers lined up behind the gate. Tar Boy, owned by Ted Zornow of the Rochester area, went to the front for driver Levi Harner. He yielded to the imported mare Arania. Then the heavy favorite Bye Bye Byrd powered to the front for Clint Hodgins and appeared to be the winner. In the homestretch, however, the Kiwi pacer Apmat rallied and thrust his neck in front to win.

Yonkers continued to welcome international pacers to the Hilltop oval for competition against the best of North America, but the international pacing simply wasn't as appealing to the media or the public as the trotting extravaganza staged at Roosevelt. No single horseman exemplified the success of New York metropolitan racing more than Billy Haughton, a native of Gloversville in central New York. He set up shop in the Big Apple after World War II and quickly came to dominate racing at Roosevelt and Yonkers. He had boundless energy, an intuitive sense with horses and a gift for attracting and retaining owners that made other trainers envious.

Haughton also had a first-rate staff that helped him master the destinies of so many horses. Among his assistants in the early 1960s were Al "Apples" Thomas, Clarence Martin, Bill "Bones" Vaughn and brother Dick, Irv Roberts, Carl Larsen and Joe Green.

As he approached his fortieth birthday in 1963, Haughton hit a milestone by becoming the first harness driver to win 2,000 career starts. His best year had been 1958 when he won 176 races, but there was seldom a season when he didn't win more than 100 races, a remarkable total for that era.

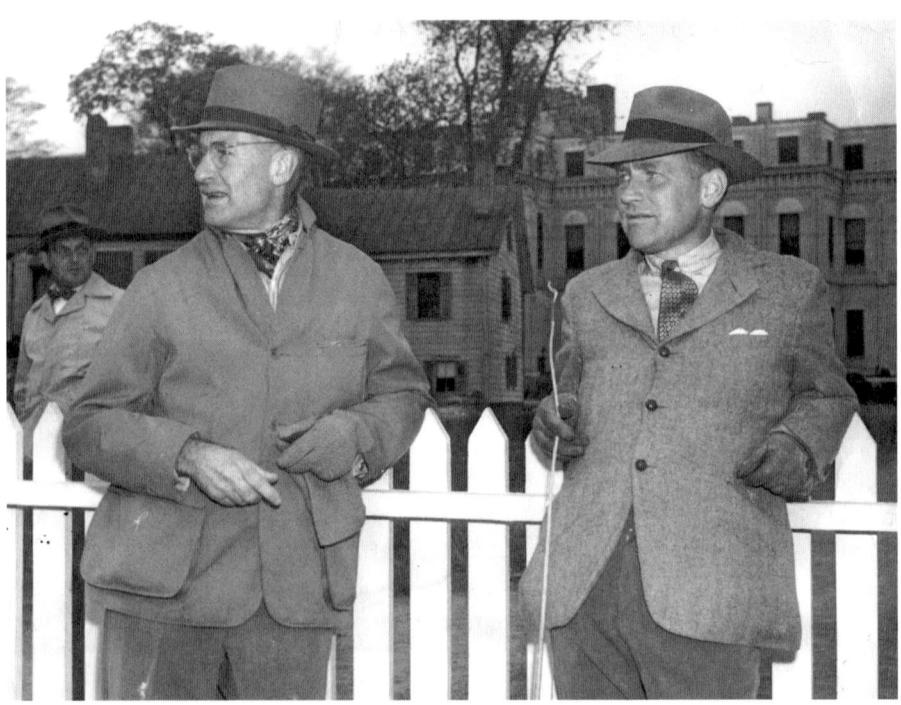

E. Roland Harriman (left) and Elbridge T. Gerry loved to sit behind the trotters that composed their Arden Homestead Stable, and they're shown here awaiting a chance to go some training miles at Historic Track in Goshen.

A History of Trotters, Tracks and Horsemen

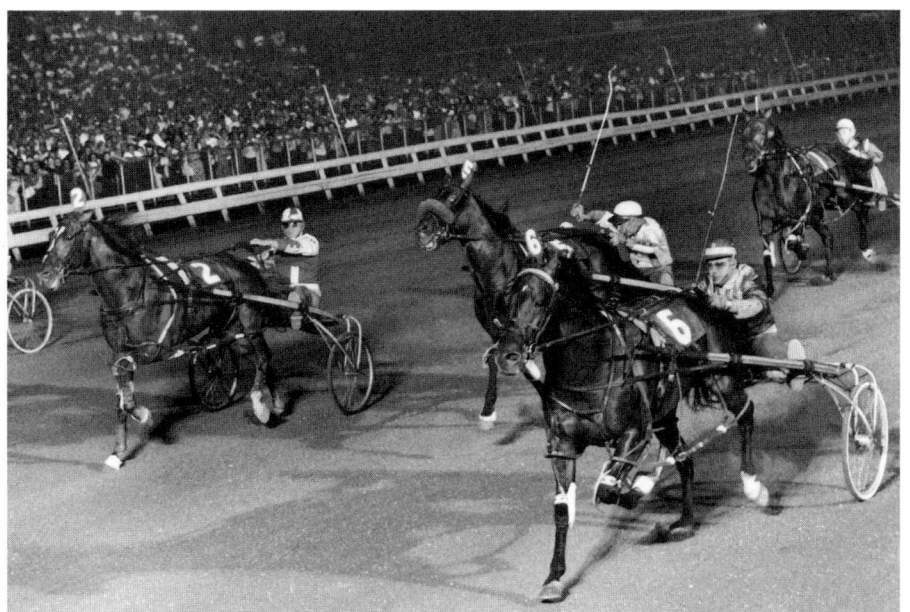

Standing room–only crowds were typical at Yonkers Raceway in the 1960s, especially when stars like Henry T Adios, driven here by Del Insko, won against the nation's top pacers. *Author's collection.*

On June 5, 1963, Roosevelt Raceway honored its brightest star with a "Billy Haughton Night" at the track. Gifts and accolades came in from all over the nation. Fellow horsemen Stanley Dancer and George Sholty gave their rival riding equipment because Haughton enjoyed riding horses as well as driving them. Roosevelt Raceway presented Haughton and his wife, Dottie, with a hunter horse for family use.

Arthur Nardin, one of Haughton's loyal owners, described Haughton to the crowd by saying to his trainer, "You have always been a gentleman, and your humility and affability have gone a long way to make harness racing a joyous adventure for [wife] Jane and me."

Haughton was mobbed by autograph seekers and well-wishers before the races started, and the fans didn't leave his side until they heard the track announcer say, "And they're off!" Haughton had to get special permission from the New York State Racing and Wagering Board for his children to attend the ceremony, but when they posed for photos, they looked like the all-American family. Billy and wife Dottie stood proudly with sons Billy Jr. (ten), Peter (eight), Tommy (six) and Robert (or "Cammie," three) and daughter Holley Ann (two).

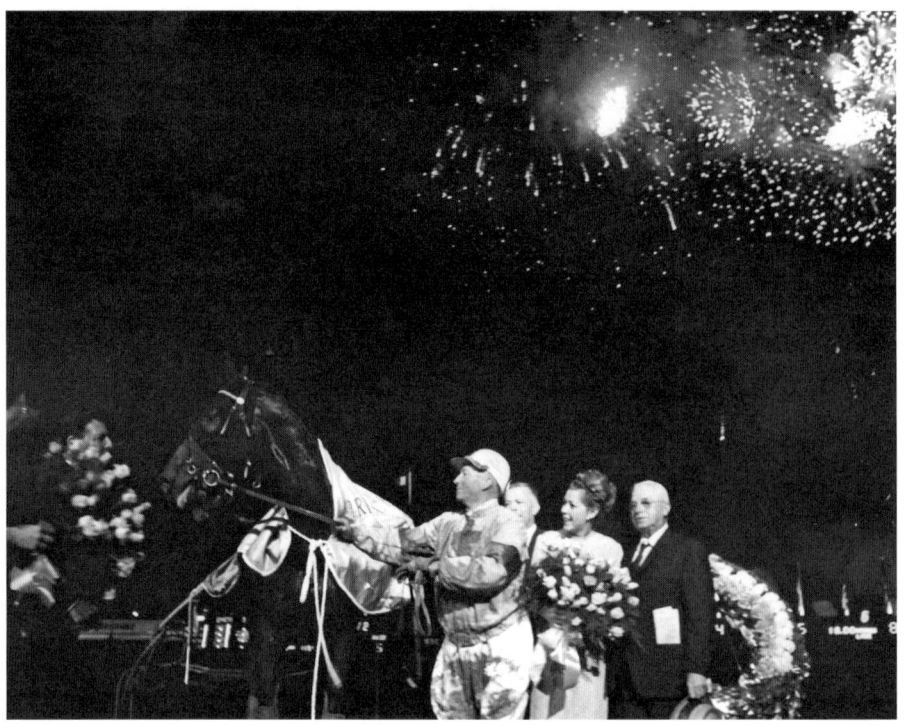

It wasn't unusual to hear "La Marseillaise" played after the Roosevelt International as French trotters often humbled the best from other countries. This photo shows the great mare Roquepine after her win with driver Henri Levesque and George M. Levy on the right.

The Haughtons were often called harness racing's version of the Kennedy family: handsome, talented and seemingly blessed. President Kennedy and his family resided in the White House when Roosevelt feted the Haughtons, but less than six months later, John F. Kennedy would meet a tragic end in Dallas, Texas. No one could have possibly imagined this at the time, of course, just as no one could have foreseen the tragedies that awaited the Haughton family in the 1980s.

There were always challenges to the racing industry, of course. Where money and wagering is involved, there will always be a suspicion that some things are not exactly kosher. In that era, when racing was still considered a major sport, it got broad and in-depth coverage from the media in the Big Apple. That helped swell the crowds for feature events, but it could turn on racing when bad news reared its ugly head.

For example, one summer, Brooklyn district attorney Aaron Koota announced that Billy Haughton was subpoenaed to testify. There was never any question of wrongdoing on Haughton's part, but his name hit the headlines. The issue was the Twin Double bets then popular at the metro tracks and the allegations that criminals were owners of the track. It soon became apparent that Koota was milking the alleged scandals for publicity and political gain. The track officials decided to call his bluff. In a full-page ad published in the *New York Times* on September 13, 1966, track officials said, "Mr. Koota: Get the guilty parties and stop making a production out of it." The ad was signed by Martin Tananbaum for Yonkers, Alvin Weil for Roosevelt and Franklin Devlin for Monticello.

For the most part, however, great things were happening across the Empire State in harness racing in the 1960s. Batavia Downs had established the Batavia Downs Colt and Filly Stakes in 1952, contested initially for modest purses but growing each year. In 1957, total purses paid at Batavia exceeded the $1 million mark for the first time.

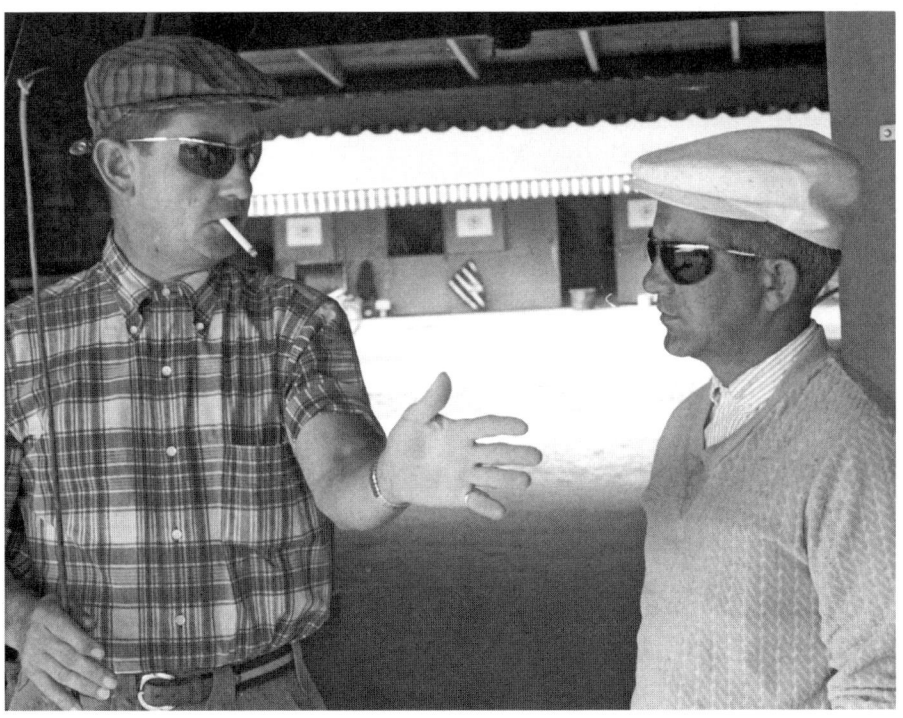

Billy Haughton and George Sholty were rivals on the track but fast friends off the track. They both campaigned large stables in the New York metropolitan area in the 1960s. Haughton was from Upstate New York, while Sholty was a Hoosier native who sought fame and fortune in the Big Apple.

Upstate at Saratoga, the half-mile oval had a reputation as one of the fastest tracks of its size, and that was always an incentive for horsemen to send their young stock north for the Battle of Saratoga Stakes. In 1968, the Saratoga track hosted the first 2:00 mile by a juvenile when Laverne Hanover looped the track twice in 1:59.4 for trainer-driver Billy Haughton. The son of Tar Heel was owned by Thomas W. Murphy Jr., son of the famous trainer-driver of early in the century.

A year later, Stanley Dancer brought Nevele Pride to Saratoga Springs in quest of a record as the fastest trotter ever on a half-mile. The record was 1:58.3, set by Speedy Rodney at both Yonkers and Historic Track. Nevele Pride didn't just beat the record; he destroyed it by trotting through a steady rain at Saratoga to cover the mile in 1:56.4 for Dancer. It was not only the fastest trotting mile ever on a twice-around, but it also was a tick faster than the fastest mile ever by a pacer on a half-mile track. Nevele Pride's record would last until 1988, when the mighty Mack Lobell came to Saratoga and lowered the speed standard to 1:56.

Attendance reached its zenith at Saratoga in 1970 as 730,283 fans attended 193 programs. Buffalo Raceway, which had opened in the summer of 1942, as the war was just starting, also became popular in the 1960s. It was situated at the Erie County Fairgrounds, only fourteen miles from downtown Buffalo. Crowds of 8,000 to 10,000 were commonplace on the weekends, and the track was popular with both Canadian horsemen and fans because of its proximity to the border.

Speaking of proximity, a trotting mare by that name was a favorite of racing fans during her outstanding career in the late 1940s. Proximity, a daughter of Protector, retired with more than a $250,000 in the bank, far more than any trotting mare.

The Buffalo track gained Grand Circuit status when the W.N. Reynolds Stakes were moved to western New York in 1957. They stayed for more than three decades and welcomed many of the best horses in harness racing during the halcyon 1960s. Certainly one of the most memorable nights in Buffalo Raceway history was when the great Bret Hanover came to down to race on July 15, 1966. Almost thirteen thousand racing fanatics packed the fairgrounds oval to see Bret do what he usually did: win easily with a typical powerhouse performance.

Business was so good during the 1960s that track management made upgrades to the grandstand, barns and paddock. Buffalo had always been a summertime track as racing was impractical during the harsh western New York winters, but in 1971, the track converted the racing surface to

A History of Trotters, Tracks and Horsemen

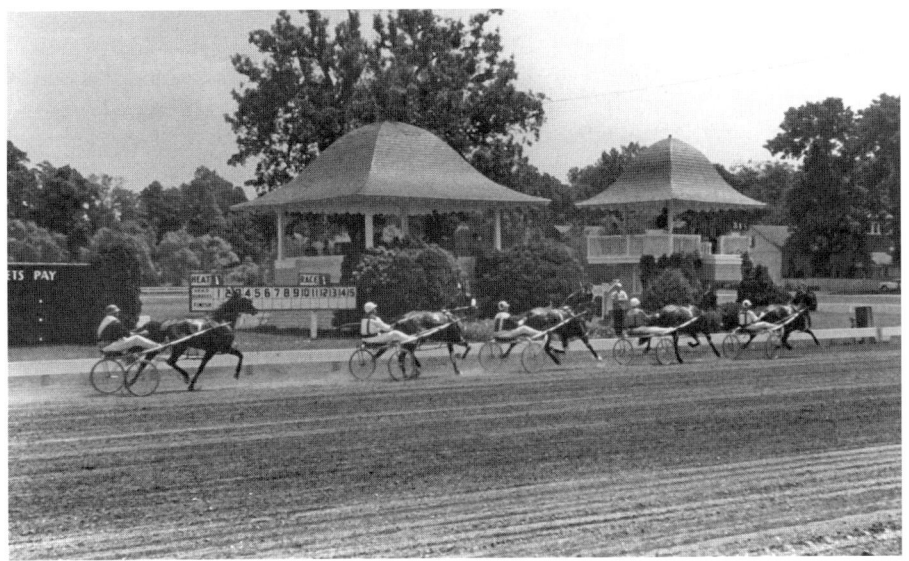

Racing at Historic Track in Goshen has long been a favorite pastime for many area residents on Independence Day weekend.

stonedust to accommodate winter racing. In early July 1972, Buffalo set a record mutuel handle of $602,821 when Stanley Dancer brought the mighty Albatross to town and flew around the half-mile oval to win.

In the Catskills, Monticello Raceway hummed along merrily thanks in large measure to the innovative promotion efforts of Allen J. Finkelson, the track publicity director. He was a big man who smoked a big cigar and hid his big heart behind a sandpaper exterior. He was quick with a quip and even quicker with an insult, much like comedian Don Rickles, but his friends knew that Allen was a kindhearted soul behind his public persona. He organized zany, off-beat promotions that even his successors at Monticello would emulate. Finkelson put on elephant races at times and often pitted star athletes in races against horses. Concerts featuring popular rock and pop stars were commonplace at Monticello.

The 1960s were certainly a turbulent time for America, but they were a time of unprecedented prosperity at New York's harness tracks. Roosevelt and Yonkers were the meccas of harness racing. Upstate in the rural areas, the harness breeders of the Empire State were making great strides of their own, most notably an innovative program that would transform racing and make New York a breeding powerhouse.

Sire Stakes Revolutionize Breeding

In the early 1950s, horse breeders in the land of Lincoln wanted to provide more lucrative racing opportunities for horses bred in Illinois. They reasoned that providing incentives for horses from the state would stimulate breeding activities there and thus prove to be a boon to agriculture in the state.

The Illinois State Fair Colt Stakes made its debut on the mile track at Springfield in 1952 with purses that astonished horsemen and owners. The purses for Illinois-bred horses dwarfed those offered to the best trotters and pacers in the Grand Circuit Stakes. Midwest horseman also loved the chance to race their young horses over the fast mile track at the Illinois State Fair, getting records far faster than they might notch at the half-mile ovals at the county fairs.

Something was afoot here. It was clearly a get-rich-quick opportunity for horse owners in Illinois, and it did not go unnoticed by breeders and owners in other states. Among those who studied the lessons of Illinois the closest were breeders in New York. After watching the popularity of the Illinois program, they put their own twist on the concept of state incentives and developed the New York Sire Stakes. It was the first such program in harness racing, and it would later become a trend that would transform the sport in many ways.

At a 1957 meeting in Syracuse, New York, breeders discussed how they could provide incentives for other breeders to patronize stallions in the state. Among the attendees were Theodore H. Zornow of Pittsford, a future president of the U.S. Trotting Association, as well as his son, Ted.

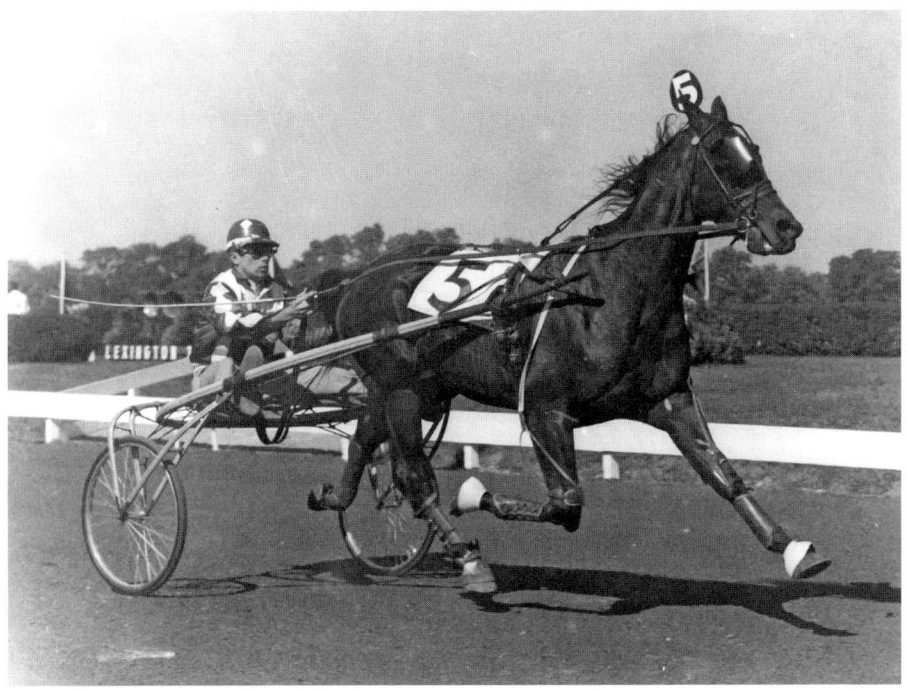

Duke Rodney was a much-feared trotter in the early 1960s. He's shown here with his Brooklyn-born driver, Eddie Wheeler. He later went to stud at Rodney Farms in western New York.

Patrick DiGennaro and veterinarian Dr. Harry Zweig were also among those present, as was Yonkers Raceway impresario Marty Tananbaum. They knew that the stallions in New York could not compete with those standing at major farms in Kentucky and Pennsylvania, so they were determined to carve out a niche for New York sires in the state with the strongest harness program.

The first New York Sires Stakes were contested at Yonkers Raceway in 1961, and the world of harness racing was distinctly underwhelmed. The two-year-old pacing filly Athena won over colts, taking the winner's share of a $7,500 purse. She was trained and driven by Levi Harner for owner Theodore Zornow and was clocked in 2:08.3. The first New York Sires Stake for trotters was captured by the filly Kate's Daughter in 2:11.3. Veteran Upstate horseman Garland Garnsey drove the winner over Riverboat, Megan and Linda's Lucky Guy. The New York Sire Stakes #1 boasted purses totaling $300,000, but the next three years, the totals jumped to $350,000 per year.

The early years of the New York Sire Stakes included events for four-year-olds. In 1963, there were two rich races for the older pacers. Senator Tefft and driver Joseph MacDonald won the first over Congress King in 2:08 at Yonkers and later at Roosevelt in 2:04.4 over Scothaven Bomber. In 1963, the first four-year-old NYSS for trotters was taken by River Boat in 2:08.2 at Yonkers, and then Ray Nibble triumphed at Roosevelt in 2:07.4. Miss Candy Bar was second in both races. Pocomoonshine was the top pacer and Broadway Joe the top trotter in the NYSS events for four-year-olds in 1964. Pocomoonshine was one of the early NYSS stars. Foaled in 1960, the trotting-bred colt blossomed into one of the best pacers of his era, winning $285,590. The following year, honors were taken by Chief Maynard and Tar Girls among the pacers and Rod Oakie and Avon Annie over the trotters.

The individual purses for the first three seasons fell in the $19,000 to $21,000 range, but by 1966, the top Empire State–sired four-year-olds were racing for almost $50,000 at Roosevelt. Those events were taken by Danny Row Gil and Hicki Hi. Danny Row Gil was another memorable

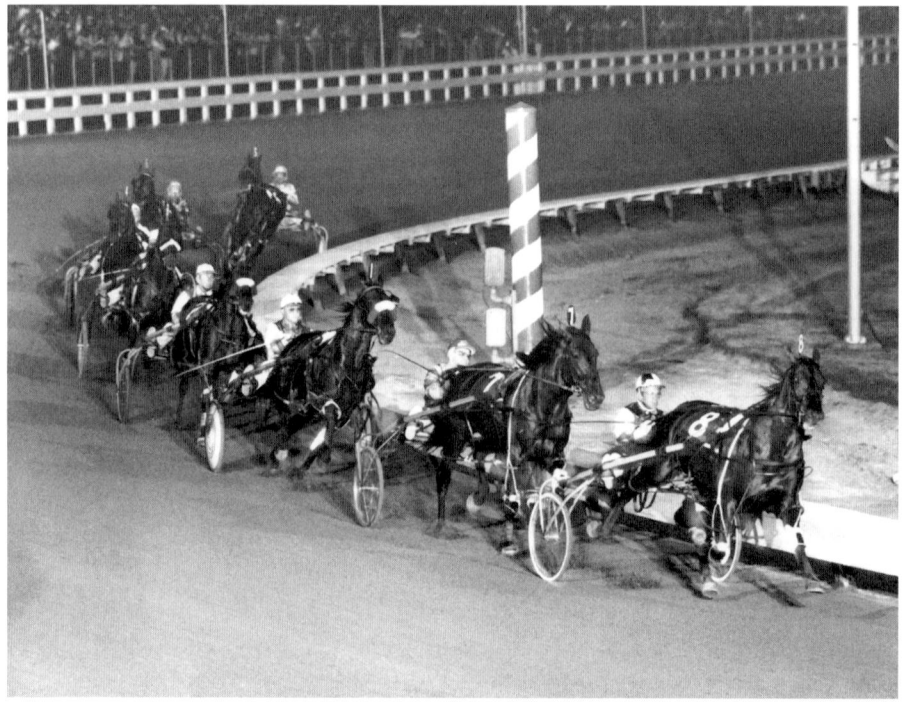

Romeo Hanover was a pacing dynamo in the mid-1960s, winning the Triple Crown in 1966. He's shown here leading the way for driver George Sholty. *Author's collection.*

A History of Trotters, Tracks and Horsemen

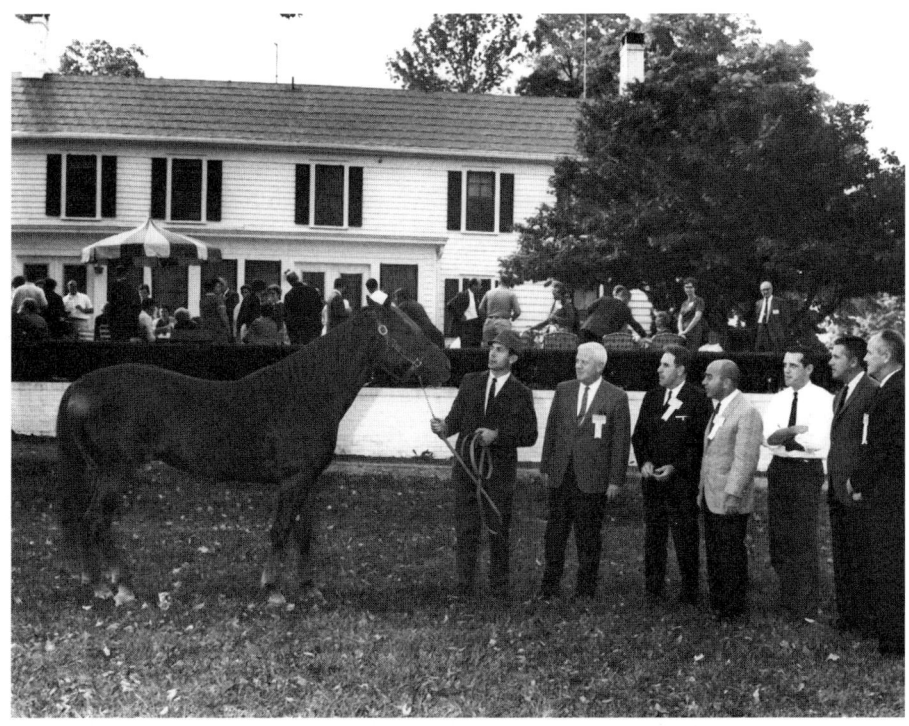

New York breeders welcomed Romeo Hanover when he retired to stud at Pine Hollow Stud in Pine Bush, New York. His accomplishments gave credibility to the young New York Sire Stakes, but he failed to leave a lasting impact as a stallion. *Author's collection.*

performer in the early 1960s. He was owned by Roy Rowcliffe, who hailed from the Elba mucklands in western New York, famed for producing outstanding onions. In Danny Row Gil, the Elba mucklands also produced an outstanding pacer. The chestnut colt stole the show on many nights in NYSS events and other races in western New York. Trainer Eldon Harner, son of Levi Harner, praised his pupil lavishly: "He's playful as a cat, likes to bite and kick a little, but he's all business on the track…He's about the nicest horse I've ever handled." In 1965, Danny Row Gil was the top pacer at the Buffalo meeting, winning the $10,000 Championship Pace, which had never been won by a three-year-old.

The early NYSS purses would pale in comparison to purses offered later. At first, breeders across the country didn't know what to make of the New York Sire Stakes events. The purses were extraordinary, but the quality of the horses sired in the Empire State didn't match the purses. It seemed like an embarrassment of riches for second-tier trotters and pacers.

Yonkers Raceway owner Marty Tananbaum could see the future of New York racing getting only better and better, so he bought and reactivated the Old Glory Sale Company. The Old Glory Sale had been the premier place to buy and sell trotters and pacers in the early decades of the century, but it had gone into dormancy. With the increase in demand for New York–sired horses, Tananbaum decided to hold the Old Glory sale sessions at Yonkers Raceway starting in 1960.

The Zornow family was one of the first to offer stallions whose offspring were eligible to the burgeoning New York Sire Stakes. They established Avon Farms in 1961, standing such stallions as Tar Boy, Concho Hanover and Maynard Hanover

Another early arrival on the Empire State breeding scene was Rodney Farms, started in Scottsville by Patrick DiGennaro to give his firebrand trotter Duke Rodney a home. The Duke was one of the greatest trotters of the early 1960s, but he was later joined at Rodney Farms by Pay Freight,

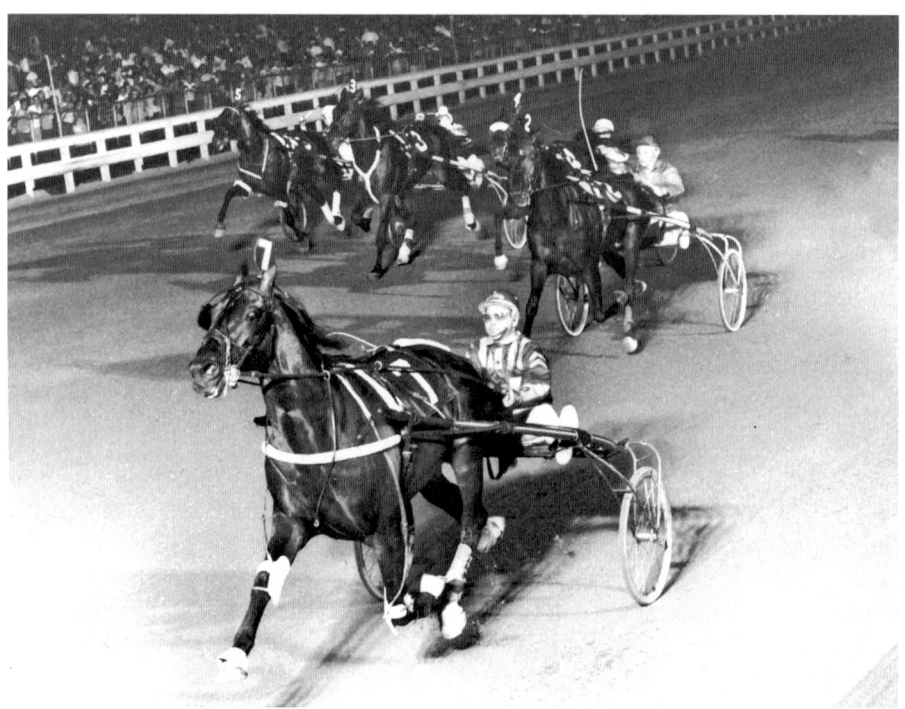

Speedy Rodney had wicked speed, but he wasn't always reliable. In the summer of 1966, though, he set a new world record for trotters on a half-mile track at Yonkers. Del Insko is in the sulky. *Author's collection.*

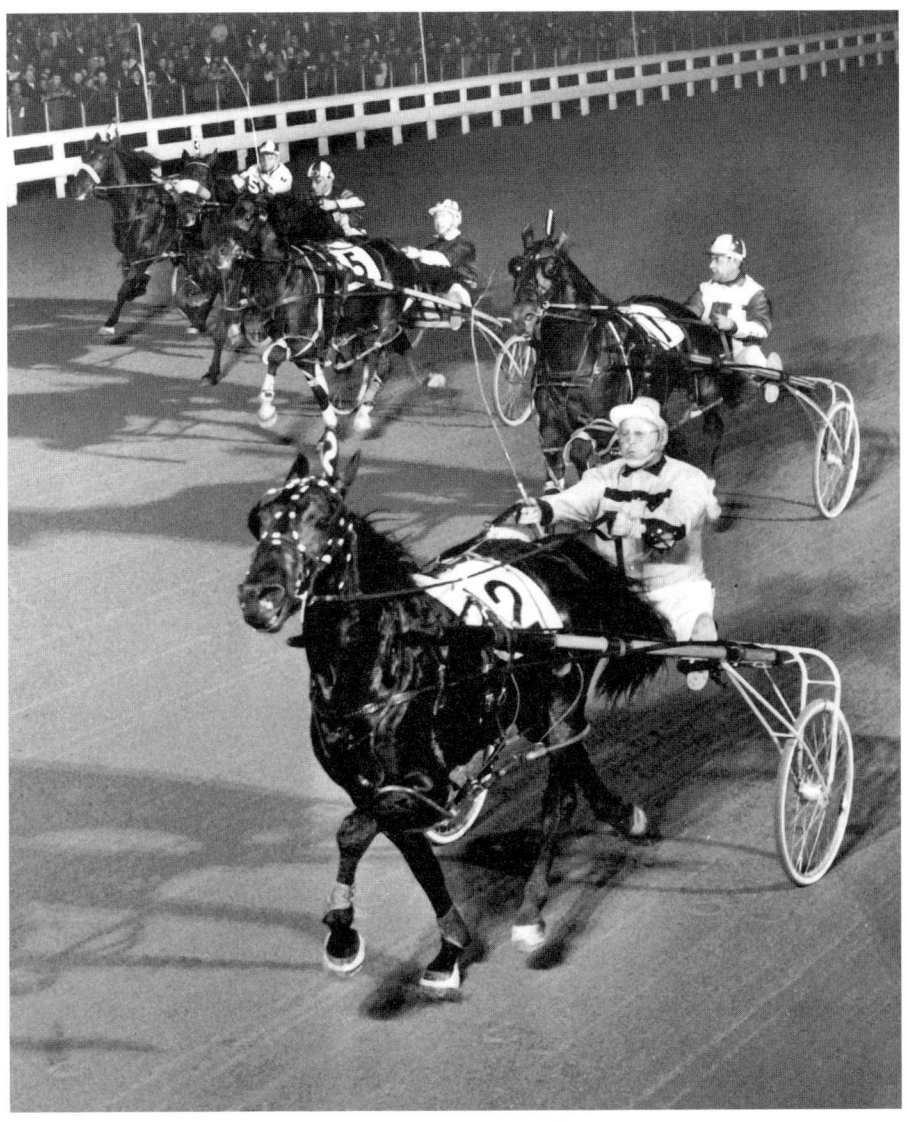

Fulla Napoleon and trainer-driver Dick Thomas chalk up another victory at Yonkers. Thomas and his father, Henry, were prominent in the postwar years in New York racing, and Fulla Napoleon later became a New York stallion. *Author's collection.*

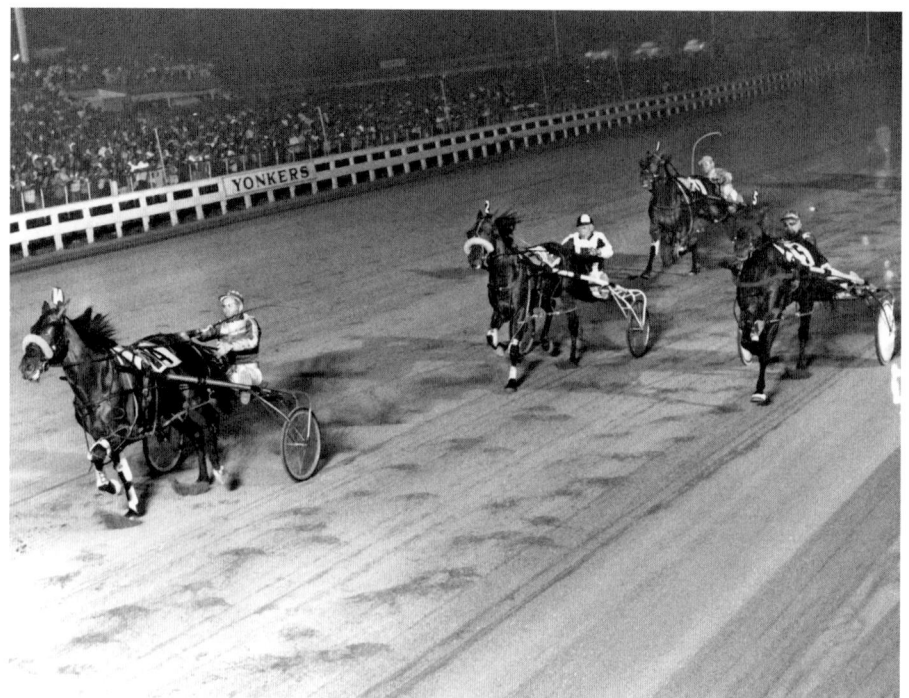

No stallion did more to give stature to New York's burgeoning breeding industry than Most Happy Fella, a Triple Crown winner in 1970. At Blue Chip Farms, he established dominance in pacing events in the New York Sire Stakes and also sent out winners in national stakes. *Author's collection.*

Olympic Hanover, Tropic Song, Grandpa Jim, Doc Hobbs, Master Yankee and Hartack Hanover.

Later, Rodney Farms plucked off a prize pacing stallion in Steady Beau, the fabled "Tennessee Stud" that had achieved remarkable success from ordinary mares while standing in the mid-South.

Tananbaum established White Devon Farm in Geneseo. Many of the White Devon products carried Minbar or Barmin as part of their names. Those represented the names of Tananbaum's daughters, Minnie and Barbara. One of the first stallions Tananbaum grabbed for White Devon was the 1965 Hambletonian winner Egyptian Candor, a son of the wildly popular Star's Pride. Another top trotter to stand at White Devon was Great Lullwater, a winner on both sides of the Atlantic Ocean. The pacers at White Devon were led by such prominent stallions as Greentree Adios, Thorpe Hanover and Adora's Dream.

The success of the Barmin and Minbars in the New York Sire Stakes gave Marty Tananbaum extraordinary personal satisfaction because he believed

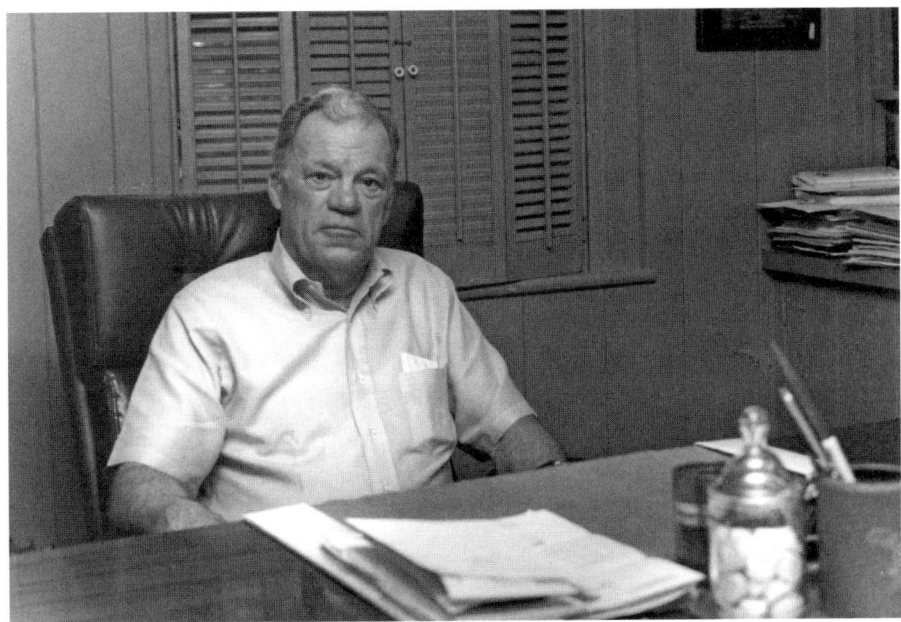

William S. Brown is credited with building Blue Chip Farms into a showplace and a major force in North American breeding. The hardworking horseman was respected by all for both his knowledge and character.

so fervently in the concept of providing incentives for young colts and fillies. In 1963, the New York Sire Stakes program listed eighty-six stallions eligible for its $400,000 prize program. The stallions were positioned in all corners of the Empire State.

The community of Albion, northwest of Rochester, was a popular location for Standardbred breeding farms. It was headed by Robinson Farm, which boasted Adios Boy, the breed's first 2:00 two-year-old, in its stud barn. He stood for a fee of $750, a significant sum in that era. His stablemates at Robinson Farm were Parading Adios ($400), Faber Hanover ($300) and Adios Leo and Dalzell (the latter pair both priced at $200). Chanceway Farm in Albion had stallions in various price ranges: Chance Play at $300, Imperial Gallon at $250 and Marvel Way at $200.

In Chester, where Hambletonian had been foaled a century earlier, Westchester Hills Farms stood Lew Burton, a brother to the famed Good Time, for a $500 fee. You could also breed to O'Brien Hanover or the trotter Tasselman for the same fee.

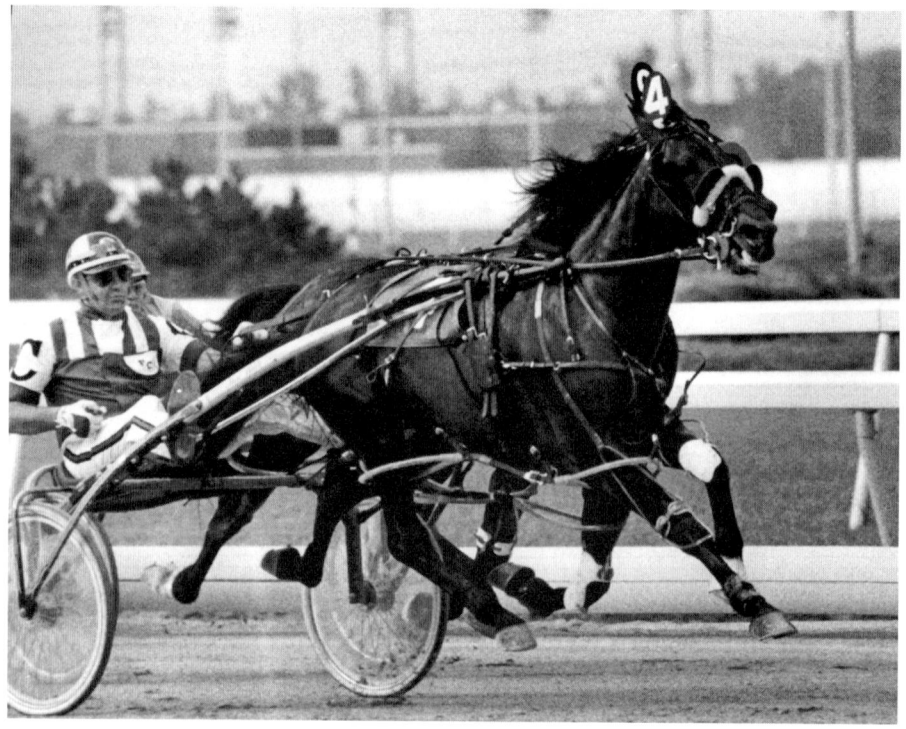

The greatest son of Most Happy Fella was the iron horse Cam Fella, a two-time Horse of the Year (1982–83). He simply refused to let another horse past him, and he passed on his toughness to his offspring.

Butternut Farm in Silver Creek, a town located on Lake Erie in western New York, offered Newport Star and Pat Rainbow at $200, as well as the Little Brown Jug winner Forbes Chief at $150. Munger Hanover was also at $150. Volomite Express and Zornow Hanover cost broodmare owners $100.

D.R. Chambers in Unadilla, a town halfway between Albany and Binghamton, was prominent in the New York Standardbred breeding scene in that era. He operated an auction company and stood such stallions as the Hambletonian heat winner Little Rocky for a fee of $300. Chambers also had the pacing stallion Calgary Byrd for $300. Other stallions he stood were Steele Hanover ($200), Pageant ($200) and Captain Woolen ($100). Scott's Clan and Terry C were both bred under a private contract. Chatham Farm, located in that community southeast of Albany, likewise had a menu of options with Grand R. Volo at $300, Razzle Dazzle at $200 and Morry Hanover at $150.

It's important to note that the records and earnings of many of these stallions were unbelievably modest by twenty-first-century standards. Morry

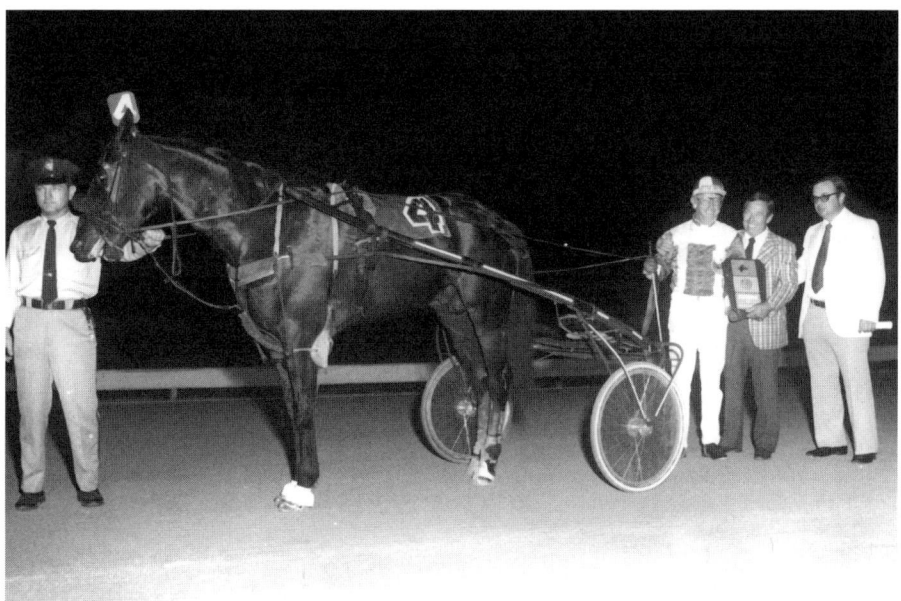

Green Speed was sired in New York by Speedy Rodney and went on to win the 1977 Hambletonian. He retired to stud in New York and sired the 1983 Hambletonian winner Duenna. He's shown with his trainer-driver, Billy Haughton.

Hanover, for example, had a trotting record of 2:08.1h as a three-year-old, and yet that was sufficient to earn him a chance in the stud.

Seaman's Farm in East Pembroke showcased Trump Hanover and Express Hall to breeders at $200. It stood a quartet of stallions—Seaworthy, Patrick Genesee, Jimmy's Champ and Prime Byrd—at $100. Mountain Nibble was offered at a $50 stud fee. Wallkill River Stable in Middletown grabbed a fast son of Adios, then the most dominant stallion in the sport, when it secured the services of Adios H, 1:57.4. His services cost breeders $300.

As the opportunities expanded, so did the breeding farms. Dan Gernatt developed a successful stud farm in western New York. The names of most of these pioneer New York Sire Stakes stallions are now long forgotten, but they were important in the development of the New York Sire Stakes. It was rare, however, that their offspring could compete with the colts and fillies sired by stallions standing at major breeding farms.

One exception was the trotting stallion Sharpshooter, whose progeny dominated divisions in the NYSS events. He sired the very successful brothers Fine Shot and Gunner, as well as standout fillies like Geranium and Duchess Rose. If you wanted to win the trotting events in the New

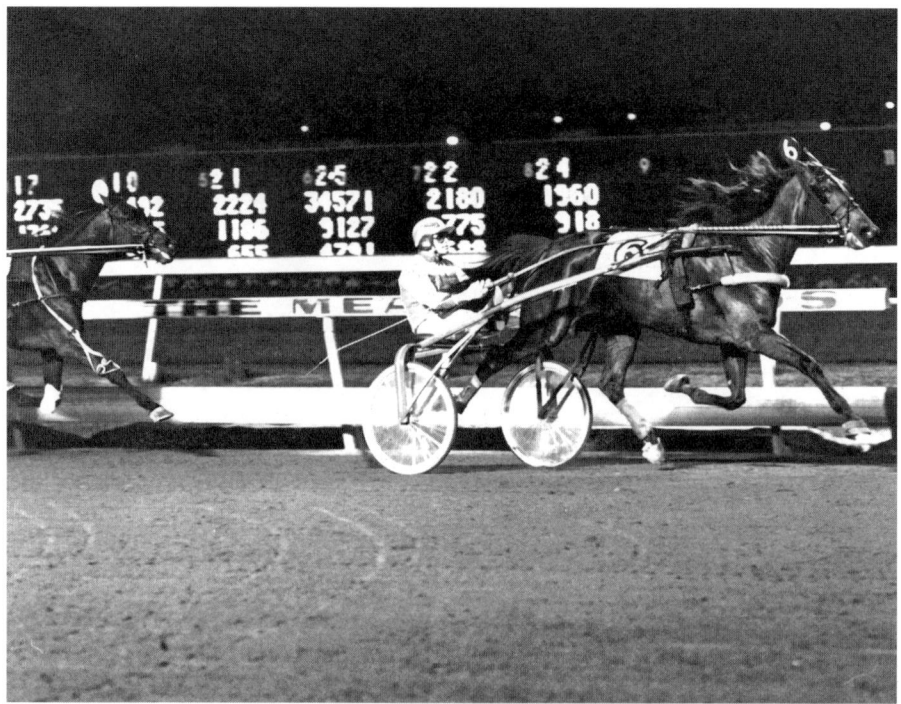

Fancy Crown was sired by Speedy Crown in New York, but she proved that she could take on the best in North America when she was named Horse of the Year in 1984.

York Sire Stakes in the 1960s, you wanted a Sharpshooter in your stable. It was as simple as that.

A turning point in New York Standardbred breeding came in the summer of 1965 when the state assembly passed the Laverne Law. This created the Agriculture and New York State Horse Racing Development Fund, which has administered the New York Sires for almost half a century. The law was keyed to a change in the manner of computing breakage on betting. It seemed insignificant to many, but it would yield $4 million. The State of New York would take half the new money, but the bulk of the remaining money would go to the New York Sire Stakes.

The Laverne Law also provided money for racing at the New York State Fair and for improvements and repairs in buildings at agricultural fairs. New York breeders immediately recognized how this would revolutionize racing in the Empire State and strengthen the state's agricultural base. (It was such an epic achievement that the following year, Hanover Shoe Farms named one of its 1966 foals Laverne Hanover after the sponsor of the landmark legislation. The pacing colt Laverne Hanover went on to achieve greatness on the track.)

Also in 1964, Robert Glasser, chairman of the New York Harness Racing Commission, pushed strongly to structure cooperation between the state's Standardbred breeders and youth in 4-H organizations. Breeders responded enthusiastically, and Glasser relied on S.W. Sabin, a professor at Cornell University, and the 4-H Extension Livestock at Cornell.

In 1964, New Yorker Morton Finder and partners purchased a fire-red yearling colt named Romeo Hanover for $8,500 and then watched him become a superstar pacer, winning the Triple Crown in 1966. When Romeo retired from racing a few years later, he found a home at picturesque Pine Hollow Stud, a new breeding farm located in Pine Bush, not far from Goshen. This Romeo wasn't lonely because the Pine Hollow Stud barn was quickly filled with the world champion trotter Speedy Rodney and later with superb performers such as Fulla Napoleon, Truluck and Songcan.

Pine Hollow's stallions represented a new level of excellence in the Empire State and signaled that other breeding farms had to kick it up a notch if they hoped to remain competitive. Concurrent to the arrival of Pine Hollow on the New York breeding farm, a Wall Street businessman named Oscar Kimelman bought a magnificent tract of land outside Wallkill and established Blue Chip Farms, named for the stocks that enabled him to find extraordinary business success. Oscar Kimelman didn't go second class. He wanted only the best in his stallions and mares. The trotting stallion All Aflame was one of the first to move into the Blue Chip stallion barn. He had been a talented trotter at times, but Kimelman knew that he would have to do better in the stud barn to make the impact he anticipated.

He did so. In late 1969, Blue Chip acquired Overcall, then the leading older pacer in North America. Overcall ran roughshod over his foes that season, winning all of his twenty-two starts and yet still losing Horse of the Year honors to the trotter Nevele Pride. Overcall had been a juvenile stakes star in 1965–66 and matured into an unbeatable free-for-all, a rare feat. He was also a virtual complete outcross to the flood of Hal Dale and Tar Heel blood then prevalent in pacing pedigrees.

Not only did Blue Chip have a new kid on the block in Overcall to start the 1970 breeding season, but Kimelman also made a bold move by acquiring the twenty-five-year-old Gene Abbe from Pickwick Farms in Ohio. Many people scoffed at the move, wondering how the old stallion would cope in a new environment. But Gene Abbe had a few aces up his sleeve.

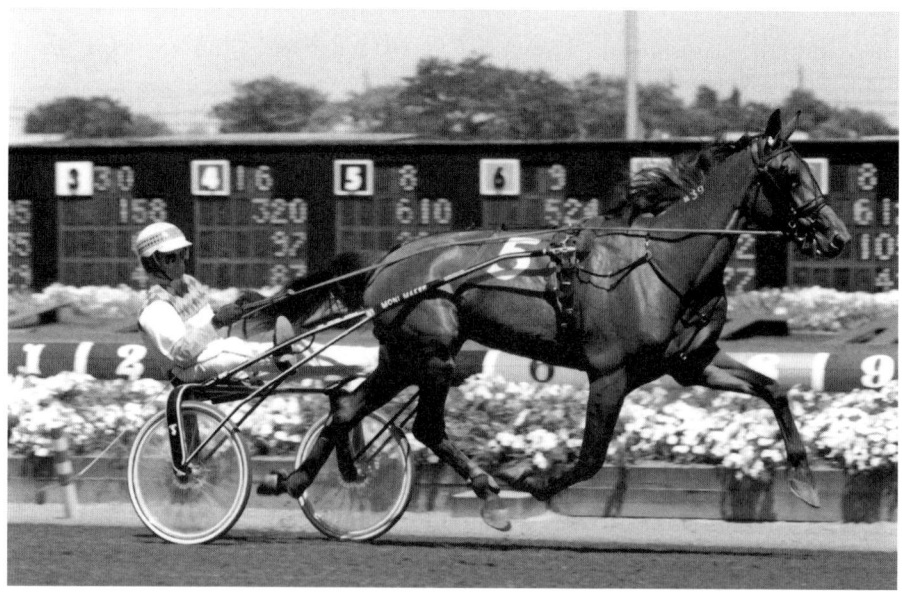

There have been many great trotters sired in New York but perhaps none better than the beloved Moni Maker. She graduated from the New York Sire Stakes to beat the best in North America and Europe. She then set a record for trotting under saddle with jockey Julie Krone.

Without question, one of the shrewdest moves that Kimelman made to boost the stature of Blue Chip was to secure the services of William S. Brown Jr. as the farm manager. Brown had served in a comparable role at Castleton Farm in Kentucky's Bluegrass for more than a decade and was universally respected in harness racing. He was the expert that Kimelman needed to build Blue Chip into a breeding farm with national impact.

The year after Overcall and Gene Abbe arrived, Blue Chip was happy to find a stall for the 1970 Triple Crown winner Most Happy Fella. He was a son of the upstart stallion Meadow Skipper, whose first two crops had made such an impact on harness racing. More than any other stallion, Most Happy Fella would move the New York Sire Stakes into national prominence by producing pacers that could regularly compete on the national level as well as in the restricted Empire State Stakes.

Most of Happy Fella's first foals arrived in 1972, and by then, New York–sired Standardbreds were certainly making their impact on harness racing. For example, that year six of the ten richest juvenile trotters were sired in New York. They were Geranium, Wayne Eden, Lady Love Me, Flame Thrower, Walter Be Good and Envy Duke. While they were not competitive with the best in the

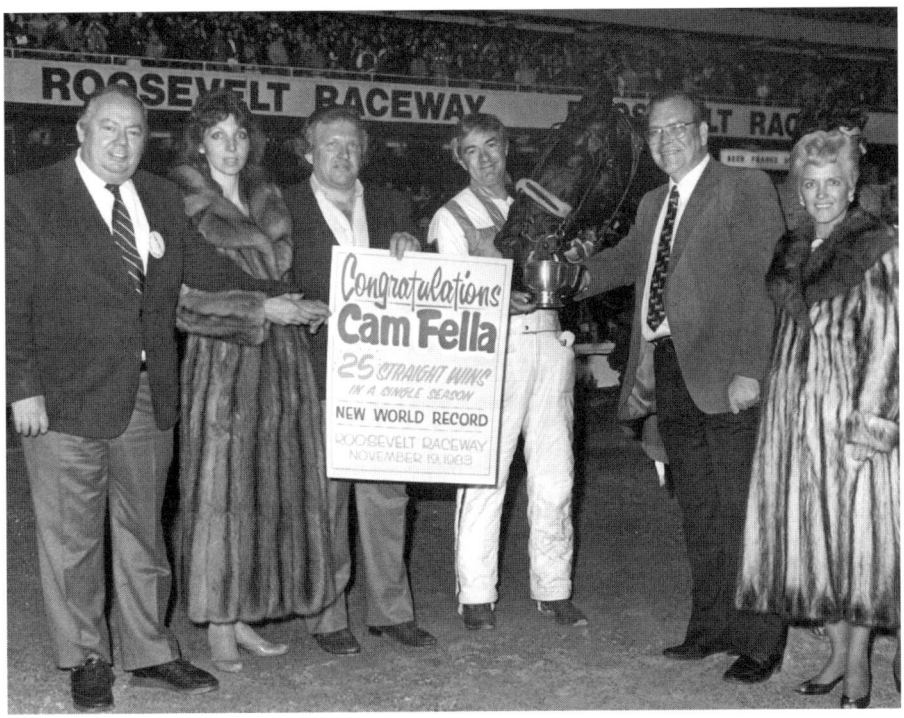

Cam Fella and trainer-driver Pat Crowe are honored at Roosevelt Raceway for winning twenty-five straight races in a single season.

sport, they were making their owners rich. The jackpots for New York were increasing rapidly. The advertised value of NYSS events in 1973 was $3 million.

Most Happy Fella's first crop included a pair of fillies that would give nationwide credence to New York–sired stars. In previous years, New York's best were seldom able to crack the top ranks of the sport. New York horses were dismissed as ordinary performers competing for extraordinary purses. The two daughters of Most Happy Fella foaled in 1972 changed that perception. Their names were Silk Stockings and Tarport Hap. Not only were they the best in the Empire State, but there were the best in North America as well. And in 1974–75, they staged many memorable duels.

Soon thereafter, Most Happy Fella sired the top-flight colt Oil Burner. Then an avalanche of pacing prowess began to flow from the young stallion. Their names were Doc's Fella, Nickylou, Armbro Aussie and the extraordinary Cam Fella, winner of fifty-eight of sixty-nine starts and more than $2 million in 1982–83. In those seasons, Cam Fella was voted Horse of the Year. Even the aging Gene Abbe contributed a headliner in Big Towner, foaled in 1974 when his sire was thirty years old. Big Towner became a widely admired half-mile-track specialist.

Most Happy Fella sired a two-time Horse of the Year in Cam Fella, but he wasn't the only horse sired in the Empire State to take top honors in harness racing.

Moni Maker, a truly magnificent mare, was sired by Speedy Crown and was a New York Sire Stakes star before becoming the toast of trotting on two continents. She was Horse of the Year in 1998–99. Gallo Blue Chip by Magical Mike and Bunny Lake, a daughter of Precious Bunny, were harness racing's best in 2001.

While New York–sired Standardbreds were gaining national stature, a researcher at Cornell University in New York was doing vital work that would prove to be a giant step forward in equine health. Dr. Leroy Coggins was focused on developing a test for Equine Infectious Anemia (EIA), a devastating disease commonly known as "swamp fever." It's transmitted by biting flies. Once a horse is infected, its system could be overwhelmed quickly by the effects, and death could soon follow. The "Coggins Test" developed at Cornell was accepted by the U.S. Department of Agriculture in 1973 and quickly became an important tool in controlling the spread of EIA and protecting vulnerable equine populations.

At the start of the 1970s, the future looked bright for New York racing and breeding. The tracks were strong and prosperous. The breeders were producing better horses every year. Everyone was optimistic. By the end of the 1970s, however, all that had changed.

Off-Track Betting and the Meadowlands Change Everything

For decades, the routine was the same. A racing fan traveled to the track, paid to park and paid admission, purchased a program and maybe a hot dog and drink and then placed his wagers. The revenue from parking, admissions, programs and concessions was all manna from heaven for track operators. Purses were based on a percentage of the parimutuel handle, but the other revenues were important income for track owners.

It was a formula that certainly worked well for the tracks, and the patrons took it as business as usual. It was left to the politicians to tinker with the status quo. In early 1965, the signs were clearly on the horizon that the concept of betting away from the track—not with a bookie but with a state-sanctioned shop—was gaining traction.

In the January 18, 1965 issue of the *Nation* magazine, Milton Wessel, a chief federal prosecutor, wrote, "New York City's proposal to legalize off-track betting moved closer to reality this January as the Democrats, its perennial champions, take control of the legislature." The stated purpose of off-track betting (OTB) was to eliminate bookies and—most importantly to the elected officials looking to fund government programs—generate up to $100 million each for both New York City and the state governments.

Wessel dismissed the idea that off-track betting would put the bookies out of business. He cited findings from raids in 1959 that showed that betting on baseball accounted for 50 percent more revenue than bets on horses. Betting was greater on football than on racing. Basketball bets and those placed on races were about equal.

Wessel also questioned if legalized off-track betting would generate the anticipated total of $200 million for the government. Robert A. Glasser, chairman of the New York Harness Racing Commission, was even more forthright in his analysis in an address before Harness Tracks of America: "It is my firm conviction that if off-track betting is adopted in my state, it would not only destroy racing, both harness and Thoroughbred, but have other disastrous effects." He continued, "Since a large portion of the public would abandon the track for the more convenient betting parlors, the results would be economic distress in the areas adjacent to and dependent on race tracks." Glasser said that off-track betting would result in job losses in the horse industry and would force some tracks to close.

Proponents of OTB said, however, that it would broaden the base of fans for horse racing and perhaps encourage new media coverage of the traditional sport. New York track officials agreed, up to a point. The crux was how OTB was implemented. They preferred that the tracks be partners in OTB, but the state government wanted to call all the shots. Track officials could see the devastation that awaited their industry and protested vehemently via the political process. They knew that the politicians coveted the revenue that OTB could generate for government coffers. Track officials said simply that any OTB plan that "takes customers away from the track without fair and adequate compensation endangers racing as we know it." There was no question that OTB would vitiate attendance at tracks. Why bother to go to a track if you could bet at a corner shop?

The aftermath was obvious, track officials pointed out. Attendance declines would result in handle declines. Handle declines would result in purse declines. Purse declines would result in breeding declines. The entire structure that built New York racing into the best in the United States would crumble.

New York City mayor John Lindsay and the city's comptroller, Abraham Beame, countered by saying that the cash-strapped Big Apple would realize untold millions in new revenue. Horsemen and track officials in New York argued for changes in the proposal. It was an uphill battle, one doomed to failure. Efforts of the dissenters were futile. When the legislation was passed, George Morton Levy at Roosevelt Raceway had no choice but to accept fate, although he knew what an impact it would have on Roosevelt Raceway. He was a lawyer, however, with a respect for the law.

On April 8, 1971, sixty-one-year-old Philip Gross sat down on a folding chair in New York's Grand Central Station. A line formed behind him. Almost twenty-four hours later, Gross rose from his chair and plunked two

A History of Trotters, Tracks and Horsemen

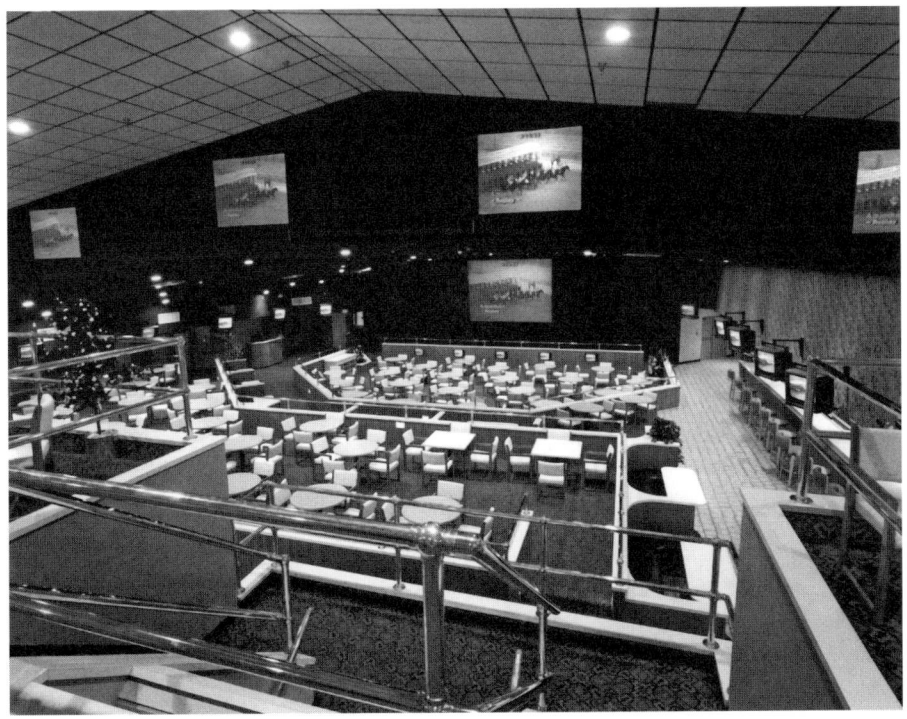

Off-track betting provided the public with a place where they could wager on races from many tracks without even going to a track. Not all the facilities were as nice as this one, and they undermined the popularity and profitability of racing.

dollars down on the nose of a pacer named Adora's Nicki, entered to race that night at Roosevelt Raceway. He was the first person to legally place a bet off track in New York. The second was Mayor John Lindsay, who put his money on a steed named Money Wise. Both men lost their two-dollar bets. What the racing industry lost in the wake of OTB in the following years was far, far greater.

Officials predicted that the first day of legal off-track wagering would total $10,000. Instead, more than $60,000 was bet off track. It did not bode well for the future. Off-track betting would be an albatross that would weigh heavily on racing in New York in the 1970s.

In 1972, New York governor Nelson Rockefeller formed a commission to study the future of horse racing in New York. It gave racing leaders an opportunity to vent their wrath on the state for undermining what had been a prosperous, profitable business employing thousands of New Yorkers and contributing millions to state coffers. In unison, they said that unless the New

York OTB legislation was repealed or drastically modified, the future for horse racing in the state was indeed bleak.

Levy was in the forefront of those offering his opinions. "I must in all candor state that even if all recommendations are enacted, there are grave reservations as to whether co-existence between on and off-track wagering can ever be accomplished in New York State," he said. Levy added that OTB would have been a strong competitor if it had a similar tax basis as the tracks, but this competitor had an unfair advantage. "In their great legislative rush, coupled with their anxiety to be more than generous to New York City, the concept of fairness and equality disappeared, and New York State played the role of Santa Claus in creating a subsidized competitor to the racing industry, with tax advantages and preferential treatment that no business could ever dare ask from any source." Statements don't get much stronger than that.

Levy pointed out that because of its favored tax status, OTB was able to give its customers a better break than the tracks could. Tracks had to put on the show and pay all the expenses, while OTB wanted to skim the cream off the tracks' revenues. "It is difficult, if not entirely impossible," he continued, "for racing to co-exist with OTB while off-course is permitted to capitalize on the racing program produced by the racetracks at tremendous daily expense."

Levy was particularly piqued by the usurious taxes on track admissions. At Roosevelt, the track paid 45 percent of its admission revenues to the state and county, while Yonkers Raceway paid a total of 50 percent. Levy was tilting at windmills, as the OTB quickly became a strong competitor to Roosevelt with its special status. There were some benefits to OTB, though. It sponsored the *Racing from New York* television show that featured Stan Bergstein, harness racing's most eloquent and informative voice. The show started in the 1970s and was a vehicle that introduced countless thousands to the exciting competition found at Yonkers and Roosevelt. Bergstein's insights and comments created thousands of new racing fans in the metro area.

Also, Monticello Raceway carded a bonanza race called the OTB Classic that was won by the filly Silk Stockings over colts in 1975. She paced in 1:57.3 over the half-mile oval to defeat colts and take the winner's share of the $230,521 purse. It was the richest race in harness racing history. Because the OTB Classic at Monticello was limited to New York–sired pacers, it provided a get-rich-quick opportunity for those with the right stuff. Oil Burner won it in 1976, and he was followed by Big Towner, the filly Happy Lady and the colt Happy Motoring. In 1980, the purse reached $306,160, and it was captured by Tyler B, a son of Most Happy Fella. The Monticello OTB Classic was later renamed the Slutsky Memorial and opened to pacers sired outside the Empire State.

Across the Hudson from Manhattan, in the summer of 1976, workers were putting the frantic final touches on a remarkable new sports facility. The new complex was called the Meadowlands, and it was set in an area that local residents knew as marshlands. The area west of the New Jersey Turnpike and east of State Route 16 was a swampy wasteland that was unused and deemed unusable. But the land was reclaimed, and from the marsh sprang a one-mile racetrack, a football stadium and a convention center suitable for indoor sports. It was operated by the New Jersey Sports and Exposition Authority. What riveted the racing world was that the track was a one-mile oval, suitable for both Standardbred and Thoroughbred racing. The only other mile tracks at extended parimutuel harness meets were in California. Most of the traditional harness tracks were half-milers or five-eighths-mile ovals.

Its location virtually guaranteed its success. The Meadowlands was closer to Manhattan than either Roosevelt or Yonkers. The new Meadowlands track had a remarkably large population base from which it could draw, and its location close to the New Jersey Turnpike made it attractive and accessible to people across northern New Jersey and the neighboring boroughs of New York City.

Officials at Yonkers Raceway and Roosevelt Raceway were well aware of the threat that a new track in the market posed. The two Gotham tracks were already weakened by the growing menace of OTB and feared what a new track a few minutes from the Lincoln Tunnel would do to their business. Not only would bettors be lured by the bright new track in Jersey, but so would the major stables. New York tracks worked behind the scenes to stymie the approval process for the Meadowlands project, but it was all to no avail.

The new track was opened to the public for its first official night of racing on Wednesday, September 1, 1976. Every seat in the grandstand was reserved and filled. All twenty-eight thousand racing programs were sold out. After 42,133 had poured through the turnstiles, the New Jersey State Police closed the gates. Racing fans found a brand-spanking-new facility with bright lights and appealing concessions and seating. They had no problem getting to the betting windows and wagered more than $2.4 million. The media also came—New York newspapers, TV stations and local Jersey media. Even Broadway Joe Namath and TV star Telly Savalas were there.

The mile track allowed for large fields, which helped boost betting and even out the tote board so that heavy favorites didn't dominate the wagering.

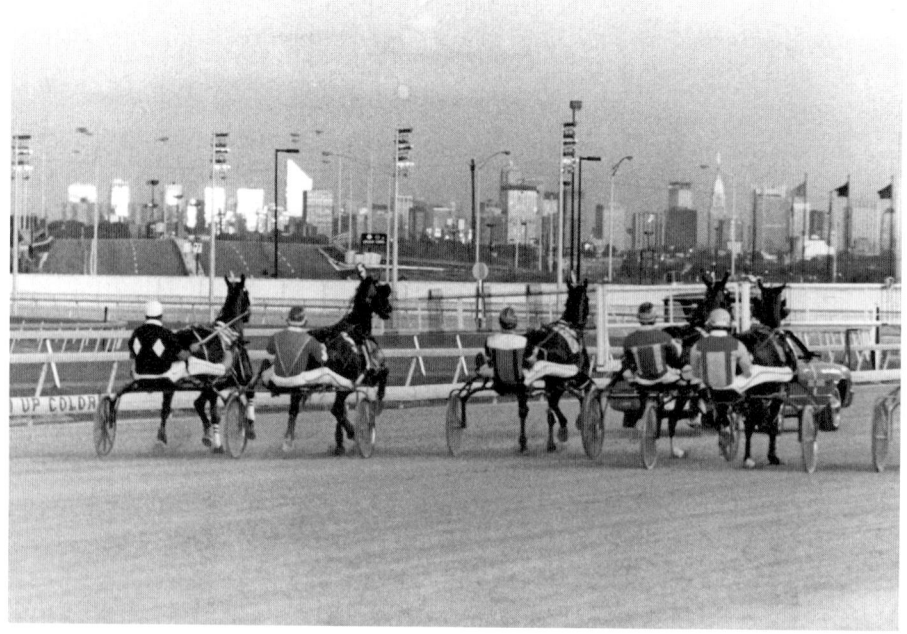

A field of horses goes behind the gate at the Meadowlands with the Manhattan skyline in the background. When the New Jersey track opened in 1976, it hurt Yonkers and Roosevelt badly.

The mile track also resulted in some astonishing times that simply weren't seen routinely at other tracks. The fastest mile ever in New Jersey before that night at the Meadowlands was the 1:57.3 mile by Albatross at Freehold Raceway. That record fell in the very first race ever at the Meadowlands when Quick Baron and Canadian horseman Ray Remmen paced to a 1:57.2 win. For the evening, the winners clocked times faster than 2:00 half a dozen times, a staggering feat in the speed-crazy sport.

Bettors loved the new track because it eliminated many of the drawbacks that they simply had to accept in half-mile-track racing. There was a definite post position bias in racing on a smaller track; horses drawing outside posts were often dismissed by bettors as having little chance. A mile track had a longer distance to the first turn and thus allowed for a more equitable start.

Perhaps the greatest difference was in the length of the stretch. The homestretch at Yonkers was notoriously short and simply couldn't compare to the long lane for homestretch heroics at the Meadowlands. Horses even well back in the pack still had a fighting chance to win at the Meadowlands. Drivers preferred mile-track racing because it was safer to

A History of Trotters, Tracks and Horsemen

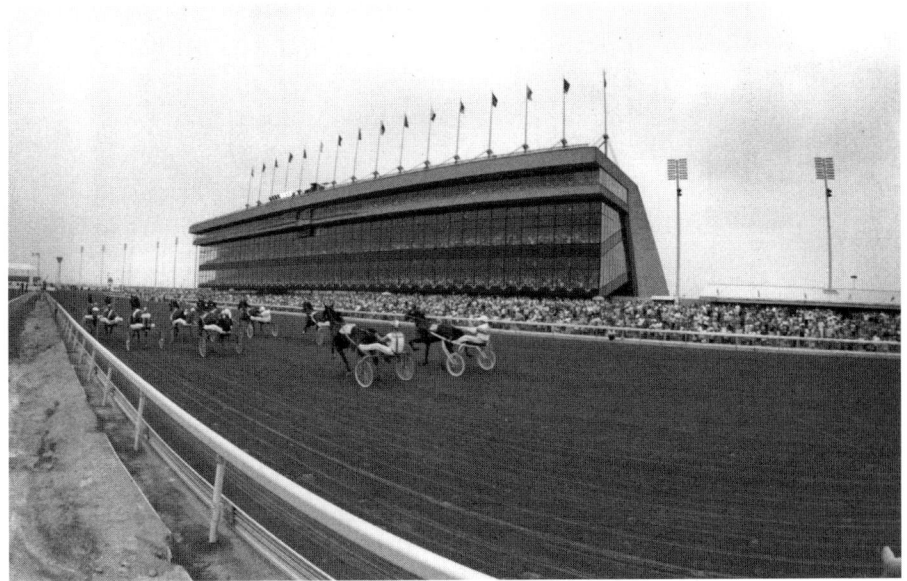

One of the key edges that the Meadowlands had over the New York tracks was its one-mile racing oval, making it more popular with bettors and horsemen than the small half-mile tracks in New York State.

go around two turns instead of four turns. That also appealed to trainers as their horses stayed sounder on a big track.

Yonkers and Roosevelt had seen the future of harness racing and realized that they were not part of it. In the mid-1970s, the new track in the Garden State wasn't the only change in harness racing. The sulky that horses pulled, which had remained basically unchanged for more than seven decades, got a significant tweak when the ends of the shafts were bent. That gave the sulky an uplifting effect on the horse when the driver's weight was in the seat. It literally lightened the load on a horse and allowed it to carry its speed further.

The twin impact of the mile track at the Meadowlands and the new sulky design came in the number of 2:00 miles recorded in North America. That clocking had always been a badge of distinction for a horse, conferring membership on an exclusive honor roll. In 1975, there had been 714 miles in 2:00 or faster. Two years later, with the Meadowlands operating a full meet and the new sulky style widely accepted, there were 2,355 miles in 2:00. During 1984, harness racing fans watched 10,899 2:00 miles.

The excitement and buzz of the new track undermined the appeal of racing at Yonkers and Roosevelt, which were already weakened by OTB.

The physical plants at Yonkers and Roosevelt, once the most opulent in harness racing, were beginning to fade and look worn. The comparison to the Meadowlands was not favorable to the New York tracks.

What Yonkers and Roosevelt still had, of course, was the tradition of such great events as the Messenger, Cane Pace, Yonkers Trot, Dexter Cup and other classic stakes for young horses. Half of harness racing's Triple Crown events were contested on the twice-arounds at Yonkers and Roosevelt. Even the appeal of those events would be diminished by the parade of new races at the Meadowlands that made the purses elsewhere look paltry. In 1980, the Meadowlands Pace carried a purse of more than $1 million, but the Woodrow Wilson for freshman pacers offered a jackpot of more than $2 million. These were events in which a horse could make its entire career with one victory. Owners and trainers found the jackpots irresistible.

Competition from the Meadowlands and the ongoing toll of off-track betting finally ended racing at Roosevelt Raceway. In the summer of 1988, the plug was pulled on harness racing's "dream track." What had once been the most modern and stylish track was now yesterday's news. The real estate that Roosevelt occupied on Long Island was increasing remarkably in value, and it was worth more for development than for a racetrack that was losing money.

The closure of Roosevelt Raceway seemed to signify a dismal future for harness racing in New York, and racing there certainly suffered in the decade of the 1990s.

Renaissance of Racing

Each generation has at least one moment indelibly etched in its collective memory. For the Greatest Generation, it was that Sunday morning in December 1941 when Pearl Harbor was attacked. For baby boomers, it was the day when President Kennedy was assassinated. For any American born before 1990, it was simply 9/11. September 11, 2001, was a day that changed America as planes brought down the World Trade Center towers in Manhattan and crashed into the Pentagon and into a field in Pennsylvania. Nearly three thousand people died that fateful day.

New York City was at the epicenter of the tragedy and suffered incomprehensible losses in lives and property. The heartbreaking process of rebuilding would take years and billions of dollars. A month after the attacks, the New York General Assembly expanded gaming laws in an effort to generate revenue for the rebuilding process. As part of the legislation, the state gave the go-ahead to video lottery terminals (often synonymous with slot machines) at racetracks. The slot machines would be under the supervision of the New York Division of the Lottery.

The legislation was the unwanted silver lining in the dark cloud of the 9/11 attacks. Racing had been declining in New York and in other states, and the prospect of added revenue from racing's share of slots revenue was a life saver. The first track to seize the opportunity that the legislation offered was Saratoga Harness, the Upstate half-miler that had opened its doors for racing fans six decades before the 2001 attacks. In February 2003, the Saratoga County Board of Supervisors voted to allow video gaming at the historic track. The facility was then renamed the Saratoga Gaming and

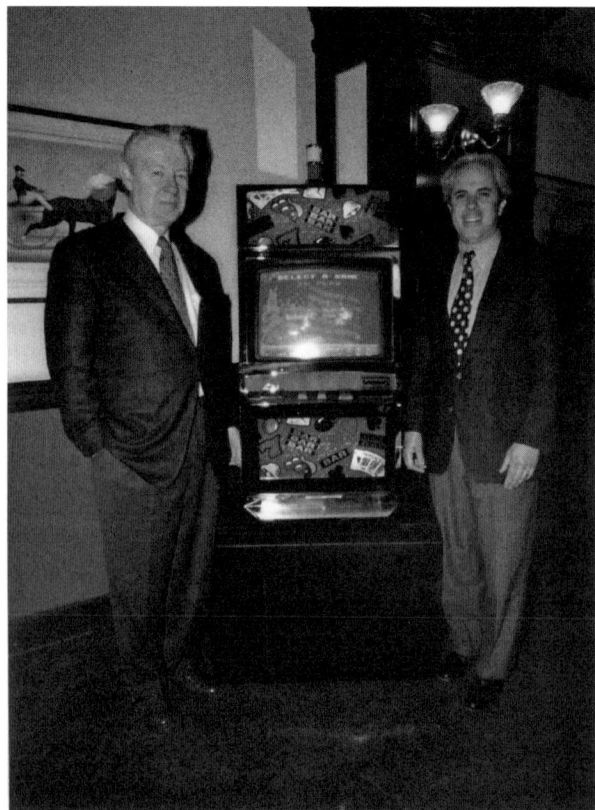

Timothy Rooney (left) and General Manager Bob Galterio developed the Empire City Casino at Yonkers, which welcomed enormous crowds. Revenues from the gaming made Yonkers the track with the highest purses in harness racing.

Raceway, and the gaming machines were opened for business on January 28, 2004. More than ten thousand guests crowded the "racino" (the newly coined term to denote a combination racetrack and casino) to be among the first to have some fun.

Business was so remarkable at Saratoga that a forty-five-thousand-square-foot expansion opened on May 1, 2007, and gave patrons 1,700 machines for their pleasure. Seeking to round out the amenities, Saratoga opened a buffet restaurant and a Vegas-style nightclub. The advent of slots promised purse increases, and that promised higher prices for yearlings. Breeders recognized that immediately.

Blue Chip Farms had long been the leader in New York State, and it added two stallions just in time to take advantage of the explosion in New York Sire Stakes lucre for colts and fillies. The first was Credit Winner, a tall, dark and handsome trotter sired by American Winner. Credit Winner was a remarkably consistent colt over two seasons on the track, finishing first, second or third in twenty of his twenty-three starts in 1999–2000. As a freshman, Credit Winner won three times in nine starts and improved as the season progressed. He was trained by Swedish star Per Eriksson and driven carefully in his starts by Jim Meittinis and John "Sonny" Patterson.

In fourteen starts as a three-year-old, Credit Winner compiled a 6-5-1 slate. He was a fast-finishing second in the Hambletonian behind Yankee Paco, closing from ninth place in the final quarter to finish just three-quarters of a length behind at the wire. A month later, Credit Winner was second in the World Trotting Derby, but he got his chance to shine in the Kentucky Futurity, which he won in straight heats, avenging his Hambletonian defeat by Yankee Paco. Credit Winner closed his career by finishing second in the Breeders Crown. Placed in the stud at Blue Chip, he proved popular with breeders and attracted ample books of mares. From his first crop came the fast Farmer Jones and the standout filly Twin B Senorita. His second crop was even better because it contained the world champion Chocolatier, a winner of more than $1.3 in his career. That same crop contained the precocious Here Comes Herbie 3 (1:52). Credit Winner was clearly established as a sire of high merit.

After the passage of legislation giving New York tracks the opportunity to open slots facilities, two more important stallions took up residence in New York. Blue Chip landed Bettor's Delight, a smallish son of Cam's Card Shark that was not only fast but also as handy as a Swiss army knife. Over the course of two seasons at the racing wars, Bettor's Delight engaged in many memorable struggles with his rival, Real Desire, and often got the upper hand. Bettor's Delight won the Breeders Crown and Governor's Cup as a two-year-old, defeating Real Desire in both events. That was enough to make Bettor's Delight the champion juvenile pacer of 2000. He had earnings of $804,661 with half a dozen wins in ten tries. He was even tougher the following year. He won the North America Cup at Mohawk, his base track in Ontario. Then he and Real Desire staged a ferocious duel in the Meadowlands Pace, with Real Desire a neck ahead at the wire.

The Little Brown Jug was contested just nine days after the terrorist attacks of September 11, and the atmosphere at the Delaware County Fairgrounds in Ohio wasn't the same as usual. Normally, the prospect of another slam-bang battle between Bettor's Delight and Real Desire would have brought anticipation to a crescendo, but instead racing fans had other concerns on their minds. In the Jug itself, Bettor's Delight thumped Real Desire in both heats to take the coveted trophy back to Ontario. Bettor's Delight won the next match in the Tattersalls Pace at the Red Mile, but Real Desire gained revenge by winning the Breeders Crown at Mohawk. Bettor's Delight then entered the stud at Blue Chip.

While the rookie pacing stallion Bettor's Delight was getting acclimated at Blue Chip, the veteran trotting stallion Conway Hall was relocating to Morrisville College in the central part of the state. He had bred 485 mares in his first three seasons at Walnut Hall Limited in Kentucky, but he was moved to Morrisville for the 2002 season. It proved to be a well-timed transfer.

While in Kentucky, Conway Hall sired the 2004 Triple Crown winner Windsong's Legacy and the fast filly Pizza Dolce. Their accomplishments and the winning ways of other sons and daughters of Conway Hall gave breeders ample reason to patronize Conway Hall once he set up shop in the Empire State at Morrisville College. Morrisville College's Equine Science program was based in a bucolic setting in the Finger Lakes Region in central New York, southwest of Syracuse. Students from around New York and other states came to Morrisville to get a well-rounded education and to specialize in equine care.

Conway Hall was just one of many Standardbred stallions that stood under the care of the college's staff and equine science students. Over the years, other top-rank stallions sending forth winners from a base at Morrisville College have been Space Shuttle, RC Royalty and Cash Hall.

In 2004, after Bettor's Delight and Conway Hall became New York residents, another rookie pacing stallion arrived at Blue Chip, and a veteran trotting stallion relocated to the Empire State—the hobbled newcomer on the scene was Art Major and the trotting veteran 1997 Hambletonian winner Malabar Man. Art Major joined Bettor's Delight at Blue Chip Farms after a career in which he won thirty-two races in forty-nine trips to the starting gate. He was developed by trainer Chris Ryder and got better over his three seasons of racing. As a sophomore, Art Major scored twenty victories in thirty-one starts and banked more than $1.5 million. He was remarkably consistent as a four-year-old in 2003 as he had eight wins and three seconds in eleven tries. He added another million bucks to his bankroll and took a 1:48.4 mark at the Meadowlands.

As impressive as Art Major's consistency was, it still fell short of the remarkable career of Malabar Man. He raced fifteen times as a freshman, winning thirteen of his races. The following year, he won thirteen times in sixteen tries, including the Hambletonian. Malabar Man was trained by Swedish star Jimmy Takter but driven to his victory in the Hambletonian by his breeder and owner, Mal Burroughs, a New Jersey businessman. His remarkable triumph in the Hambo was only the second time in history that the winning trotter was steered by an amateur reinsman.

Malabar Man went to stud in New Jersey in 1998, and his first few crops contained such noted trotters as Power to Charm (Hambletonian favorite in 2003), Elegant Man, Armbro Barrister and Malabar Maple. It was obvious that New York was a happy hunting ground for another trotting stallion, so Malabar Man set up shop at Winbak Farms starting with the 2004 breeding season. Winbak moved into New York as part of an ambitious expansion program that saw the Joe Thomson–led breeding colossus establish a presence in virtually every major jurisdiction in North America.

In 2007, Morrisville College welcomed to its stud barn Cash Hall, the fastest trotter ever on a half-mile track by virtue of an astonishing 1:51.3 time trial at Delaware, Ohio, the previous year. Cash Hall had been a $300,000 yearling and had a gold-plated pedigree and a solid conformation. He loomed as one of the favorites for the 2004 Hambletonian but finished third behind Windsong's Legacy. His performances at ages four and five were not up to the promise he had shown as a sophomore, but his world-record time trial propelled him into prominence, and he bred 351 mares in his first two seasons at Morrisville.

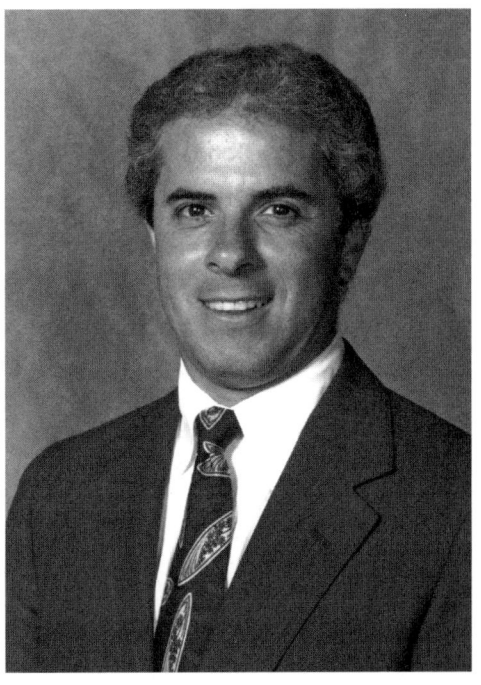

Bob Galterio masterminded the addition of a gaming facility at Yonkers Raceway. The track had to be closed temporarily for construction, but customers loved the Empire City Casino and flocked to play the gaming machines.

The arrival of fresh new faces in the stud barns in the Empire State altered the breeding landscape, and most of the spoils on the trotting side went to the offspring of Credit Winner and Conway Hall, while the sons and daughters of Art Major and Bettor's Delight came to dominate pacing events.

In addition to standing stallions, Morrisville College conducts an annual yearling auction each September to bring together sellers and buyers. The overwhelming majority of yearlings are by New York sires, so it's a necessary stop for any owner or trainer seeking to make a splash in the New York Sire

Stakes. The sale began modestly but grew with the expanding purses and racing opportunities in New York. The average sale price jumped to past five figures for the first time in 2008 when 197 yearlings sold for an average of $10,774.

Not only were new stallions coming to New York, but a new harness track also appeared on the scene. New York real estate mogul Jeff Gural acquired Tioga Downs, a shuttered Quarter-Horse racing facility in the Southern Tier, thirty miles from Binghamton near the Pennsylvania line. The track had carded Quarter-Horse races for three years but never turned a profit for the owner. He pulled the plug. In his youthful days, Gural had been an avid horseplayer and regular fan at Roosevelt Raceway on Long Island. He knew harness racing and understood it from the bettor's perspective. As he became successful in business in New York City, Gural gained a new perspective on racing as an owner and breeder.

When slots at New York tracks became a reality, Gural seized the opportunity to purchase what was left at Tioga Downs. Groundbreaking for improvements was begun in the summer of 2005, and the track was ready for racing and gaming customers one year later. Gural was no Pollyanna. He had witnessed the declines in the popularity of horse racing (both Standardbred and Thoroughbred) from the days when he spent many nights at Roosevelt Raceway. He was quoted in the *New York Times* as saying, "Like it or not, the reality is that without slot machines, most racetracks would probably disappear." Complicating matters was that Tioga Downs had a very limited population base from which to draw its customers. The flip side was that there wasn't much else in the way of entertainment around Nichols, New York.

The new Tioga, built at a cost of $40 million, was a track for the times. It wasn't a huge, overbuilt palace designed for the crowds of twenty-five thousand or more that had once flocked to tracks. Gural and the gaming company that was a minority owner with Gural recognized that those days were gone and weren't coming back. Instead, they built Tioga into a modern, compact facility where racing and gaming could live in peaceful coexistence. That's what made Tioga so appealing to many people in the harness racing business. Although slots were very much part of the facility and a big part of the revenue stream, racing was not treated like the poor country cousin to be hidden and kept out of sight. Instead, Gural showcased the racing at Tioga. He knew that the slots would generate an ample cash flow, but he wanted harness racing to be a draw, too.

Racing wasn't the only way Gural planned to lure people to the track. Concerts and special events were very much part of the calendar. Tioga's marketing was aggressive—track staff left no stone unturned in searching for customers. Gural wasn't out to get rich at his own personal Field of

A History of Trotters, Tracks and Horsemen

Dreams, though. He was already rich, thanks to a successful career in real estate. What he wanted to do was make the harness racing successful, and he wanted the track to be a good member of the local community.

In 1990, after more than twenty-five years in existence, the New York Sire Stakes decided that it should crown a champion each year. Thus it began a "Night of Champions" to bring the best in the state together for a final slugfest after a long season of races across the state. It would be the crowning point for New York's racing for the youngsters sired in the state. The big night was first held at Yonkers Raceway.

Popular trainer Larry Rathbone and driver Abe Stoltzfus took top honors in that inaugural Night of Champions as they combined to win two championships with freshmen fillies. The trotting lass Sherbie's Lady scored in 2:03, while Stoltzfus and Rathbone claimed another victory with the pacing filly Lexie, a winner in 1:57.4. The legendary Hall of Fame horseman Stanley Dancer, then in the twilight of his career, scored a victory driving Gift Box to victory in 2:03 over freshmen male trotters. The top juvenile colt pacer was Cocktail Talk, driven by Cat Manzi for trainer Steve Elliott. His winning mile was timed in 1:59.1. The fastest Night of Champions winner in 1990 was Young Wave, a sophomore pacing daughter of Niatross trained and driven by Steve Smith to a 1:57.2 win. That was faster than the 1:57.4 win registered by Justin Private in beating the three-year-old males for trainer Gordon Roselle and driver Rod LaFramboise.

The European influence was apparent in the trotting events for three-year-olds. Sambuca Lobell, trained and driven by Pekka Korpi of Finland, triumphed in 2:01.2, while Berndt Lindstedt of Sweden drove Camelia Lobell over the filly trotters in 2:00.3. His fellow Swede Bjorn Berglund trained the winner.

Everyone in New York realized that the landscape would change when Yonkers Raceway opened its slots facility. The track underwent extensive renovations and even closed for a while to allow construction to move forward. In 2004, that resulted in the Yonkers Trot being moved to Hawthorne Race Course in Chicago. Yonkers was the harness track closest to the New York metro area, and everyone knew that it would generate incredible sums for purse accounts. By the time the Empire City Casino at Yonkers opened for business, however, it was obvious that public support for racing had waned so badly that crowds were sparse and on-track wagering was minimal. That was as true in New York as it was across North America. Horse racing had clearly lost favor with the public. The addition of gaming at New York tracks came just in time.

Harness Racing in New York State

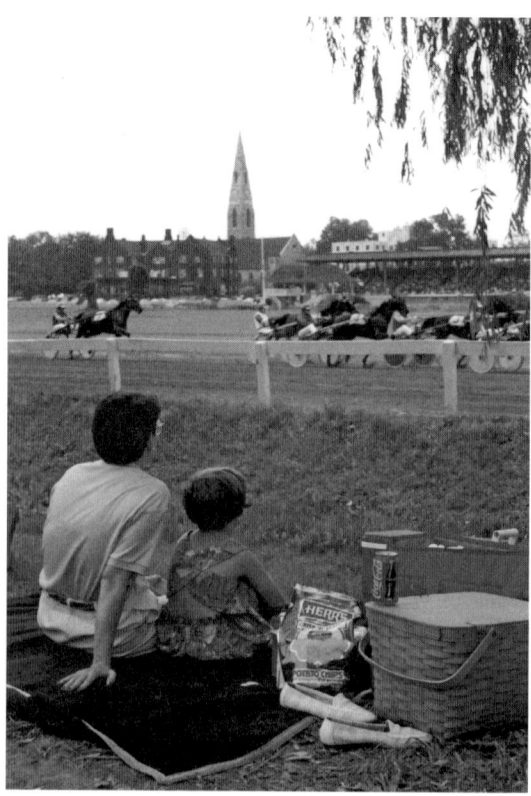

The enduring appeal of New York harness racing is captured in this scene at Historic Track in Goshen.

The declines certainly weren't limited to just harness racing. In 2011, Belmont Park, the Thoroughbred track that hosted the third leg of the Triple Crown, finished its season with an average attendance of 3,811. This was in a facility that was designed to accommodate 70,000 racing fans. Many harness tracks would have loved to have an average attendance of 3,811, as their figures were far lower.

The arrival of slot machines in New York was like the cavalry arriving in a western movie: it was just in time to save the day. Without the expanded gaming opportunities that slots provided customers, it's clear that many tracks would have closed. Instead, they thrived. People poured into Yonkers Raceway at night, but most headed for the slot machines and not for the betting windows. The revenue from the machines did not just keep racing alive, it enabled Yonkers to soar far above the Meadowlands in purse offerings. It was clearly a case of role reversal. For almost thirty years, horsemen had aspired to race at the Meadowlands and shunned Yonkers; now the shoe was on the other foot.

In 2011, Yonkers Raceway paid purses of more than $67.5 million, while the Meadowlands offered $37.7 million. The average purse at Yonkers was $22,587, while Meadowlands, despite some million-dollar events, averaged $12,456. While Yonkers was clearly at the top of harness racing in purses in 2011, Saratoga Raceway also offered more than $15.8 million to owners, and Monticello Raceway fell just short of reaching $10.0 million in purses paid.

A History of Trotters, Tracks and Horsemen

Still, not all was picture-perfect in New York racing. It never was that way, and even slots couldn't make some problems go away. Early in the summer of 2012, the New York State Racing and Wagering Board suspended harness trainer Luis Pena for 1,719 violations of drug rules. The incidents took place in 675 races in New York State. The news hit the harness world like an earthquake. Many people had suspected Pena of skirting the rules because he demonstrated such a remarkable ability to improve horses once they came under his care. Still, his horses did not have any positive post-race tests. In fact, Yonkers Raceway had excluded Pena from racing there for several months in 2011 but then reinstated him.

The New York State Racing and Wagering board cooperated with the New Jersey Racing Commission to summon the records of veterinarians who treated Pena's horses at his stable's base in the Garden State. The U.S. Trotting Association immediately took action to suspend Pena's membership. Pena said that he was innocent of the accusations, but the damage to racing's reputation was already done. The confidence in harness racing took a severe blow.

Shortly thereafter, New York governor Andrew Cuomo said that in his plan to expand gambling across the Empire State, racetracks would not have exclusivity on casinos. At the same time, Cuomo acknowledged that the racinos at tracks would have a difficult time competing against new, full-scale casinos. That immediately raised questions about the future of racing in New York. "I do not think the racinos have any claim for primacy," said Governor Cuomo. He further went on to say that the racino situation in New York as of 2012 was a "scandal."

No one expected that the funding from the slot machines would last forever, but Cuomo's announcement had a chilling impact on the state's racing industry. It was obvious that New York harness racing—and Thoroughbred racing, too—would face yet another challenge and an uncertain future. That was not a new situation in the Empire State. Horsemen and track operators in the state had overcome many obstacles in their path in previous decades. There had been other scandals and challenges that seemed to spell doom in the history of New York racing. Each time, racing overcame the barriers it faced. The enduring appeal of horses and the competitive spirit of those who race them always overcame any challenges.

Some said that harness racing in New York might be nearing the finish line, but those familiar with the history of the sport in the state cautioned the naysayers, "Don't bet on it." Purses continue to rise in 2012, and breeding activity is another sign that the sport should be strong for many decades into the future.

Empire Builders

It would certainly be foolish, not to mention impossible, to attempt to list all the native New Yorkers who have made significant contributions to harness racing since the nineteenth century. Such a list would simply be too long, so what follows is a list of some New York–born individuals who helped build the sport into an industry and sustain it, both in their native state and across the nation.

For decades, New York has been a magnet for horsemen and owners seeking to achieve success at the pinnacle of harness racing. To quote Frank Sinatra, "If you can make it there, you can make it anywhere." They came from Ohio, California, Illinois, Canada and elsewhere to showcase their skills under the bright lights of the big cities. Those people are not included in this list, as the focus is instead on natives of the Empire State who made contributions over many decades.

Carmine Abbatiello

Known to racing fans as simply the "Red Man" because of his silks, Abbatiello was one of the top drivers on the Roosevelt-Yonkers circuit for many years. A native of Staten Island, he drove the winners of 7,170 races, and horses he steered earned more than $50 million. He was a quick-thinking and aggressive reinsman. He started working under his brother, Tony, and developed into a driving ace at Monticello before moving on to stardom in the Big Apple. In 1968, he passed the one-thousand-win milestone in his career and then just kept on going. In the 1970s and '80s, he could be relied on to crank out $2–3 million in purse earnings. He was inducted into the Living Hall of Fame in 1985.

A History of Trotters, Tracks and Horsemen

Frank A. Antonacci
This Long Island businessman sealed his immortality in early 1970 when he purchased an unraced freshman trotting colt from trainer Howard Beissinger. The colt was named Headin and Heelin after a rodeo event, but Antonacci renamed his purchase Speedy Crown. He watched with great pleasure as Speedy Crown won the Hambletonian and then went on to an extraordinary career as a sire. Antonacci himself (often known as "Big Frank" in the sport) left a lasting impact on harness racing through his Crown Stable that included many champion trotters. He passed away in 2004.

Guy Antonacci
Known throughout harness racing as "Sonny," Antonacci was proud of his association with Hambletonian winners Lindy's Pride, Probe, Harmonious and Victory Dream. He was a cousin of Frank Antonacci and had a son named Frank who assumed an influential role in harness racing. Sonny established Lindy Farms in the 1970s and passed his love of harness racing on to his sons Frank and Gerry, as well as to the next generation.

His greatest horse was the international trotting star Moni Maker, a two-time Horse of the Year. She earned more than $5.5 million. She was sired in New York by Speedy Crown. Sonny Antonacci was inducted into the Living Hall of Fame at the Harness Racing Museum less than a year before his passing in 2001.

Charles Backman
Born in 1824 in Pittstown, Backman used the earnings from his successful business career in New York City to establish Stony Ford Farm in Campbell Hall, New York, during the Civil War. He recognized the greatness of Hambletonian as a progenitor and stood several of his influential sons at stud. Backman often welcomed U.S. president U.S. Grant as a visitor at his farm.

C.K.G. Billings
Born in Saratoga Springs in 1861, Billings became president of People's Gas, Light & Coke Company in Chicago. He had inherited a love of harness horses from his father and owned many champions, such as Lou Dillon, Uhlan and William. His horses never raced for purses but instead were exhibited for speed only. Billings loved to drive his own horses, and the C.K.G. Billings Amateur Driving Series is named in his honor.

John A. Cashman Jr.

Cashman Jr. was born the year Roosevelt Raceway was opened and when his father was establishing a reputation as an official at the track on Long Island. The senior Cashman ultimately became the track's presiding judge, while his son was named director of racing at Roosevelt at the age of nineteen in 1959. At that time, Roosevelt Raceway reigned at the absolute pinnacle of harness racing, drawing extraordinary crowds regularly and playing host to the best horses in the world. The Roosevelt International attracted trotters from around the world and was the grandest spectacle in the sport.

Cashman Jr. also was involved in standing stallions such as Hambletonian winner Speedy Streak at Buttonwood Tree Farm in New York. He owned and operated Cashman-Magee Sale Company, which conducted auctions.

In 1980, he became general manager of Castleton Farm and later assumed leadership positions at Pompano Park and the Red Mile. For many years, Castleton Farm operated a breeding facility in the Goshen area. Cashman Jr. was inducted into the Living Hall of Fame in 1993 and had previously won the Horseman Award (1987) and the Proximity Achievement Award (1989).

Clarence F. Gaines

Gaines was extremely successful in manufacturing and marketing pet food, and his interest in animals carried over to a true passion for trotters and pacers. He established Gainesway Farm in Lexington in the 1940s and stood such stallions as King's Counsel, Algiers and Peter Astra. He was a fervent believer in acquiring broodmares with demonstrated racing class and was proud of how many Gainesway mares had 2:00 records in the post–World War II era.

Gaines took an active role in the founding of Vernon Downs in central New York, and his inquisitive mind led him to develop the plastic wheel disk for sulkies. He campaigned a high-class stable that included Hambletonian winners Kerry Way (1966) and Speedy Streak (1967), and later he enjoyed the international fame of Kerry Way's daughter, Classical Way. His son, John R. Gaines, was active in breeding and owning Standardbreds before switching his allegiance to Thoroughbreds.

Glen Garnsey

Born in 1933 on Grindstone Island in the middle of the St. Lawrence River, Garnsey learned harness racing by watching his father, Garland, a prominent Empire State horseman in post–World War II years. When Glen began driving, his soft touch and confidence in the sulky was immediately apparent. Others said that young Glen had a "million dollar set of hands."

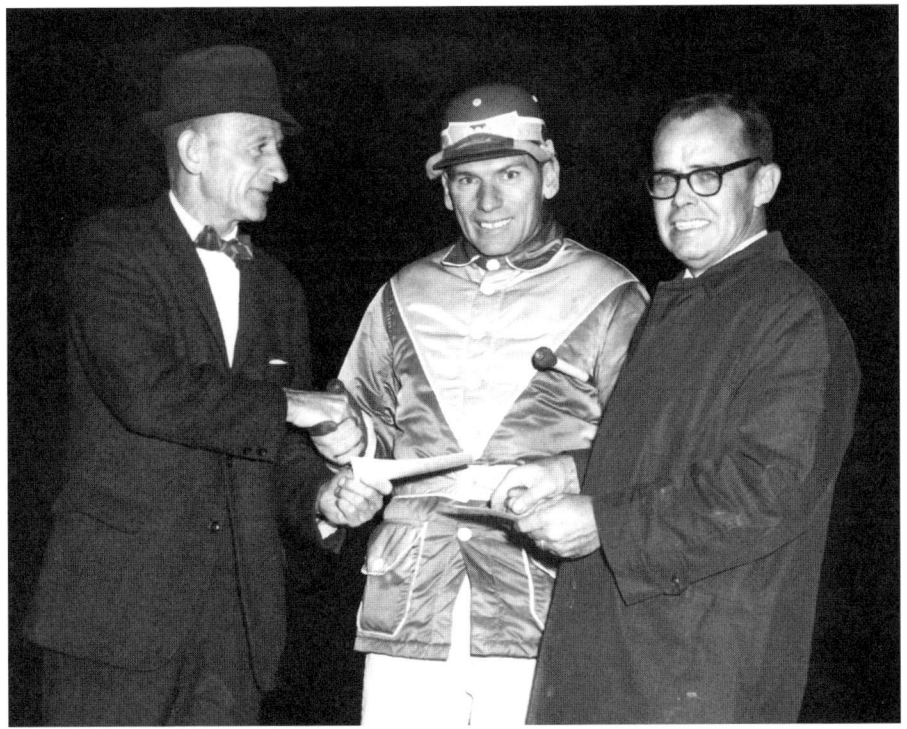

Glen Garnsey (center) was a horsemen with a "million dollar set of hands," and he used those hands to drive many great horses to major victories. On the left is Mickey McLean, race secretary at Vernon Downs. *Author's collection.*

Garnsey began winning more and more races in New York, but he wasn't winning races with large purses. He facetiously described his status in the early 1960s as "successful but starving." His talents attracted the attention of prominent Grand Circuit owner K.D. Owen, who hired Glen as a private trainer. He made such a favorable impression with the Grand Circuit regulars that he was soon hired for the prestigious position of private trainer for Castleton Farm. Ralph Baldwin, the highly respected horseman who had conditioned the Castleton Farm stock in the 1960s, was cutting back due to ill health, and Garnsey won the plum job.

Garnsey lived up to the expectations. He raced Snow Speed at the end of his four-year-old season and then began developing the Castleton yearlings. In 1970, he brought out Hoot Speed from the first crop by the Speedy Scot, the "Castleton Cannonball" who won the 1963 Triple Crown. Hoot Speed was a star freshman in 1970 and chased Speedy Crown to the wire in the '71 Hambo.

Training for a prominent breeding farm meant that Garnsey often had a stable full of females, and he proved to be a real ladies' man. He won three of the first four Hambletonian Oaks for fillies driving Gay Blossom, Colonial Charm and Berna Hanover. In 1976, Garnsey trained and drove the breed's first 1:55 freshman in Striking Image. In 1978, Garnsey trained and drove the Horse of the Year Abercrombie, later a great sire at Castleton.

Garnsey and the pacing filly Fan Hanover achieved immortality in 1981 when they dodged accidents to win the Little Brown Jug, making her the only distaffer to win the Delaware pacing classic. Garnsey later raced such stars as Delmegan, No Nukes, Incredible Nevele and Armbro Blush.

Glen Garnsey was killed in an automobile accident in Lexington in 1985 after attending a yearling auction.

Elbridge T. Gerry Jr.

It's certainly no surprise that this man took a strong interest in trotting; it was in his blood and all around him in life. His father was active in the sport and held positions of great prominence in racing both in New York and on a national level.

Young Ebby was just eleven years old when he watched Titan Hanover, owned by his father and his uncle Roland Harriman, scamper to victory in the Hambletonian at Goshen. He grew up steeped in the traditions of trotting, idolized the prominent trainers and drivers and loved watching the Arden Homestead horses trot to victory. He followed the accomplishments of such horses as Star's Pride, Florican, Hit Song, Matastar, Florlis, Geraniun, Flirth, Kick Tail and many others.

The Gerry family worked behind the scenes in many ways to preserve the best traditions of harness racing. The Gerry family's support for the Harness Racing Museum in Goshen allowed this important gem to showcase harness racing to thousands of visitors each year.

Elbridge T. Gerry Sr.

A man of monumental influence in harness racing, Gerry Sr. was a 1931 graduate of Harvard and became involved in trotting with his uncle, Roland Harriman. Gerry Sr. was also an accomplished polo player in the years before World War II. He served in the U.S. Air Force during the war. He was associated with the private banking firm of Brown Brothers Harriman for most of his life and contributed to racing in many ways. He was the first racing commissioner in New York State and was named to the

Hambletonian Society in 1947. He served as its treasurer for forty years, and the trophy in the filly division, the Hambletonian Oaks, was named in Gerry's honor in 1996.

Gerry was associated with such top trotters as Titan Hanover, Matastar, Florlis, Flirth, Kick Tail, Me Maggie, Torway and many others. He was the great-great-grandson of the Elbridge Gerry who signed the Declaration of Independence and who also served under James Madison as vice president. The term "gerrymandering" was coined in the early 1800s when Gerry was governor of Massachusetts and signed a bill that redrew district lines for elected officials.

Gerry died in early 1999, and his wife, Marjorie, died just six days later.

Jeff Gural

This Manhattan real estate magnate grew up going to the races at Roosevelt Raceway and loved spending time at the track with his friends. He later became involved as an owner and breeder and then took the major step into track ownership when he acquired Vernon Downs and rebuilt Tioga Downs near the New York/Pennsylvania state line. Both Vernon and Tioga soon acquired an enviable reputation in the sport for their progressive management and active promotion of racing.

When the Meadowlands track in New Jersey was threatened with closure by the state of New Jersey in 2010, Gural stepped in at the last minute to avoid disaster. He had to overcome enormous obstacles in his way to obtain the operating lease, but he never wavered in his commitment to save harness racing at the Meadowlands. His actions brought him an outpouring of appreciation from people in harness racing across North America. His ownership style at Tioga and Vernon has often been cited as an example for the ideal partnership between racing and gaming interests at a track.

Gural has been an active breeder and owner of trotters for many years.

E. Roland Harriman

Many people feel that without Roland Harriman, there would be no harness racing today. In the late 1930s, when the sport was fragmented and lacking public support, it was Harriman who brought the various interests together to form the United State Trotting Association. Before that time, racing regulation was disjointed and in the hands of competing associations—the American Trotting Association, the National Trotting Association and the United Trotting Association. The registration of horses was handled by the Trotting Horse Club of America.

Harriman used his standing in the sport to unite the diverse elements into a cohesive body just in time for the explosion of nighttime parimutuel raceways that opened in the 1940s.

Harriman's interest in trotting was a passion he inherited from his father, E.H. Harriman, owner of the Union Pacific Railroad. The elder Harriman had a stable of trotters at the turn of the century. Roland grew up around horses and enjoyed driving trotters as an amateur. He came to share his father's love of horses and took up breeding and owning. His Arden Homestead Stable had two starters in the first Hambletonian in 1926 and won the big race in 1945 with Titan Hanover and in 1973 with Flirth. His wife, Gladys, also took an interest in horses and drove several of the Arden Homestead horses to fast record miles in exhibitions.

Roland Harriman died in early 1978 at age eighty-two, and the sport he saved mourned his loss.

James C. Harrison

Along with John Hervey, Harrison was the master harness historian and journalist of the twentieth century. His passion for harness racing began in the 1930s and continued until the 1990s. A native of Port Jervis, he began covering the Hambletonian in nearby Goshen. He went to work for the U.S. Trotting Association in the early 1950s and began contributing articles to *Hoof Beats* that were deeply appreciated by breeders, owners and trainers.

Lawrence B. Sheppard lured Harrison to Hanover Shoe Farms in the late 1950s where he served as Sheppard's right-hand man. He was brought back to the USTA by Executive Vice-President Don Millar to undertake the monumental task of researching and writing *The Care & Training of the Trotter & Pacer*. That 1968 volume was an instant classic.

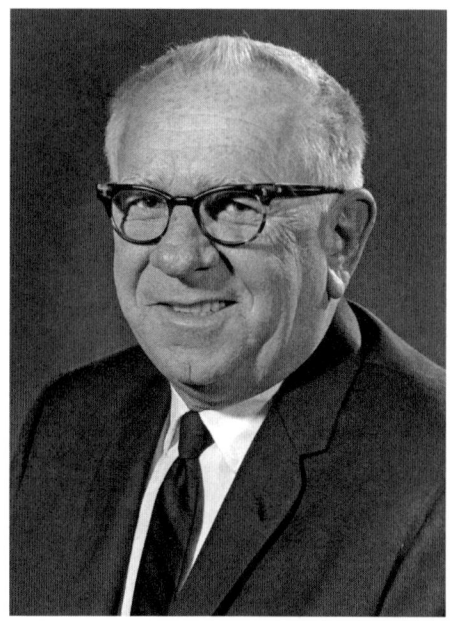

Journalist James C. Harrison, a native of Port Jervis, combined a comprehensive knowledge of horses and pedigrees with an excellent command of the English language. His articles provided insight into harness racing history.

A History of Trotters, Tracks and Horsemen

Harrison also wrote pedigree articles for *Hoof Beats* and then was hired by Lana Lobell Farms to manage its growing Pennsylvania facility. He retired from that position to live out his remaining years along the New York/Pennsylvania border. He was a regular feature during the Grand Circuit races at Historic Track.

WILLIAM R. HAUGHTON

Billy Haughton was harness racing's perpetual motion man. No one had more energy and more talents than the native of Gloversville in central New York. He burst into national prominence in the post–World War II years when he was still in his twenties. His talent was obvious to his peers, who often used him as a catch-driver. He established his own stable in the metropolitan area, and like Topsy, it just grew and grew.

In 1955, he ventured to the Delaware County Fairgrounds in Ohio for the first time and walked away that night after driving Quick Chief to a Little Brown Jug victory. It would not be Billy Haughton's last Jug victory. That same year, he won the first Cane Futurity with Quick Chief. It would not be Billy Haughton's last Cane victory. The next year, Haughton won the first Messenger Stakes at Roosevelt Raceway. It would not be Billy Haughton's last Messenger victory.

Haughton could do it all and did it all. He could train, drive and select yearlings, and he managed the largest stable in harness racing. He did this combining horsemanship with endless energy and an engaging personality. After winning his first Little Brown Jug, he added victories with Vicar Hanover, Rum Customer, Laverne Hanover and

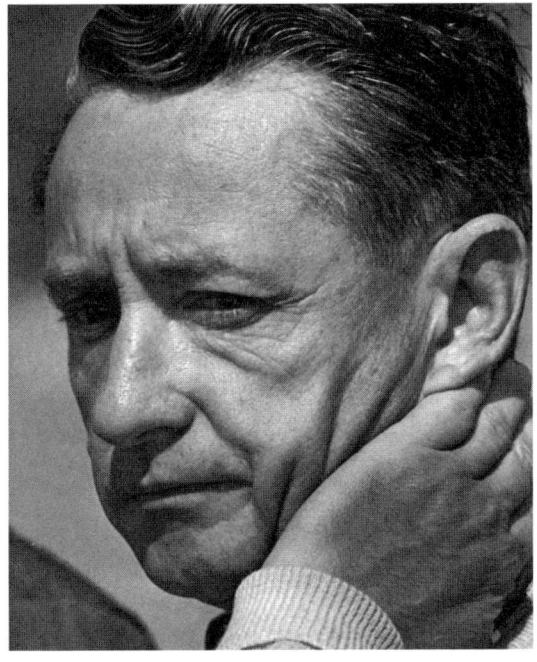

Billy Haughton was a masterful horseman who made friends for racing (and friends for himself) wherever he went. He died as a result of an accident at Yonkers Raceway in 1986.

Armbro Omaha. After his first Cane triumph at Yonkers, he added victories with Meadow Paige and Rum Customer.

Haughton won the Messenger at Roosevelt an incredible seven times: after Belle Acton came Romulus Hanover, Rum Customer, Silent Majority, Armbro Omaha, Bret's Champ and Windshield Wiper. He didn't win his first Hambletonian until 1974 with Christopher T, but then he captured three of the next six Hambos with Steve Lobell, Green Speed and Burgomeister.

His promising son, Peter, was killed in an auto accident in 1980. Another son, Tom, won the Hambletonian driving Speed Bowl in 1982.

Billy Haughton died as a result of injuries suffered in a racing accident at Yonkers in 1986. Everyone in harness racing knew that the sport had suffered an inestimable loss.

Oscar Kimelman

This Brooklyn-born bookkeeper was born in 1908 and developed a successful business helping firms get listed on the New York Stock Exchange. His business prospered and allowed him to purchase a trotter in 1965.

The horse Meadow Tarport achieved success, and Kimelman and family fell in love with the sport that was then at the peak of its popularity. He began to look for property that would make a suitable breeding facility so that he could participate in the burgeoning New York Sire Stakes. He bought a large and picturesque six-hundred-acre tract near Wallkill, not far from Goshen. The new facility was named Blue Chip Farms in tribute to the influence of Wall Street, and Kimelman's sons, Mike and Ted, joined him in his enthusiasm for racing.

Among the first stallions to stand at Blue Chip were All Aflame, Overcall and the aging Gene Abbe, brought from Ohio. The stallion that vaulted Blue Chip Farm to national prominence, however, was Most Happy Fella, the 1970 pacing Triple Crown winner. He arrived at Blue Chip about the same time that the legendary farm manager, Bill Brown, was hired to supervise the development of the new farm.

Kimelman went first class and bought fillies and mares with superior pedigrees, and soon Blue Chip was among the sport's leading breeders.

George M. Levy

Levy is recognized as the guiding force behind the success of Roosevelt Raceway on Long Island, which revolutionized harness racing when it opened an extended parimutuel meet in 1940. His achievements at Roosevelt earned him widespread respect, and they are detailed elsewhere in this book.

CATELLO MANZI

This Monticello native dominated the driving colony at nearby Monticello Raceway in the 1970s and then became one of the top catch-drivers at the Meadowlands in New Jersey during its heyday. He won the $1.1 million North America Cup in 2004 driving Mantacular. The following year, his 727 wins ranked him first among all drivers, and he was the oldest driver ever to achieve that honor. He was inducted into the Living Hall of Fame in 2002. He's driven such top horses as Winky's Goal, Pacific Fella, Harmonious and Riyadh.

CHARLES MARVIN

Born in Genesee County in 1839, Marvin grew up working with horses and served as a teamster during the Civil War. He later trained for Governor Leland Stanford in California and developed many champions such as Sunol, Smuggler, Arion and Palo Alto. He was one of the first horsemen to emphasize training young horses for speed. His book *Training the Trotting Horse* was published in 1893 and makes for interesting reading more than a century after Marvin's death in 1907.

ERNEST B. MORRIS

This tall attorney practiced law in Albany starting in 1931 and yet always found time to indulge his love for harness racing. He was born in Rensselaer in 1908 and graduated from Union College and Albany Law School. He was among the principals in the early years at Saratoga Raceway. Morris later served as legal counsel to the U.S. Trotting Association and on its board for many years.

THOMAS W. MURPHY

This Poughkeepsie horseman so dominated harness racing in the first quarter of the twentieth century that it was rumored that his middle initial of "W" stood for World's Record. That wasn't true, but it would have been fitting for Murphy, who drove many horses to fifty world's records during the peak of his career.

Jim Harrison, a journalist without peer in the postwar years, said that "Murphy was the Jim Thorpe, Babe Ruth, Red Grange, Jack Dempsey and Bobby Jones all wrapped into one." The great horseman Delvin Miller, judged to be the best harness horseman of the overall century, was proud to be known by the nickname "Murph" when he was a young man.

The horses that Murphy campaigned may not mean much to readers almost a century later, but they were headliners in their era. Peter Scott,

Peter Volo and Guy Axworthy were immortal builders of the breed, and Murphy raced them all.

After suffering numerous broken bones and injuries in racing accidents, Murphy decided to give it up and go out on top. He left after the 1927 racing season and turned to training Thoroughbreds. The rail-thin horseman developed a Kentucky Derby winner in Twenty Grand. Murphy later worked as a stock broker on Wall Street and served as an advisor to Allwood Stable in the 1950s, when he selected Kimberly Kid and The Intruder for the operation. He later purchased Bullet Hanover as a yearling and watched him win the 1960 Little Brown Jug in record time.

Murphy died in 1967 at age ninety.

HARRY E. POWNALL

Brooklyn native Harry Pownall was a talented trainer of trotters and a friend to all his colleagues in the training fraternity. He gained national prominence

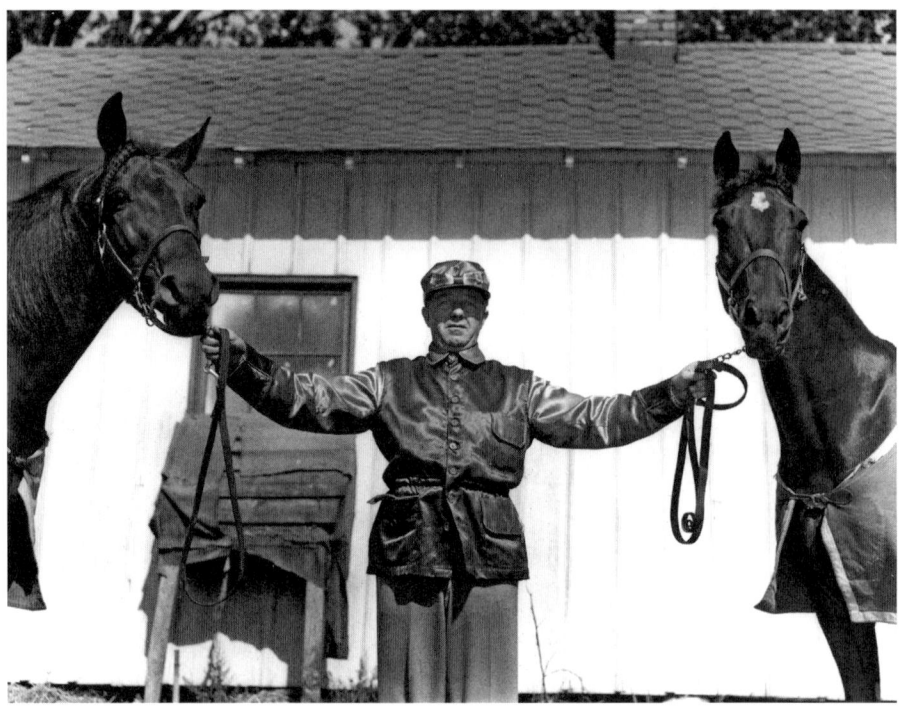

Brooklyn-born Harry Pownall was a Hall of Fame horseman greatly admired and liked by his peers. Two of his greatest trotters were Star's Pride (left) and Florican (right). They were foaled in the same year and were both outstanding on the track and in the breeding ranks.

in 1937 when he drove Farr in the Hambletonian for Billy Dickerson, the head trainer for Arden Homestead Stable.

In the 1940s, as Dickerson aged and cut back on his training duties, Pownall assumed a greater role with the Arden Homestead stock. In 1944, he struck the mother lode when he developed a package of trotting dynamite named Titan Hanover. That fall at Lexington, Titan Hanover became the first two-year-old Standardbred, trotter or pacer, to record a "miracle" 2:00 mile. (To put that time in perspective, the three-year-old Yankee Maid won the Hambletonian that same year with a fastest time of 2:04.)

In the 1945 Hambletonian, Titan Hanover was barred in the wagering. Despite starting on the outside in the second tier, Titan Hanover breezed to victory in straight heats for Pownall. After that, Pownall was a fixture in the Hambletonian virtually every year, sitting behind an Arden Homestead trotter. He drove Florican to a 5-3 finish in 1950 and was 1-3-2 with Hit Song two years later. In 1963, he once again won the opening heat, this time in a world record 1:57.3 as Florlis defeated Speedy Scot.

Pownall also developed and campaigned the speedy but eccentric Matastar, which became the world's fastest trotting stallion in a 1962 time trial in 1:55.4.

Timothy J. Rooney

Rooney served as the president of Yonkers Raceway for many years and masterminded the development of the Empire City Casino there that

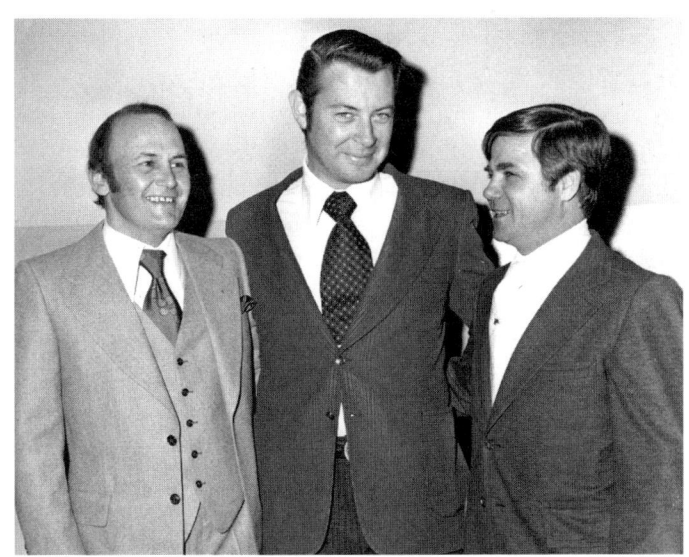

Tim Rooney of Yonkers Raceway is flanked by two of harness racing's all-time great reinsmen. On the left is Herve Filion, a winner of 15,180 races in his career, and on the right is Del Inkso, a winner of 4,753 races. All three men are members of the Hall of Fame in Goshen.

resulted in skyrocketing purses. He was active as a breeder and owner of high-class trotters and pacers for many years and operated Shamrock Farm in Maryland, which was home to both Standardbreds and Thoroughbreds. Rooney is the son of the legendary Arthur Rooney and was one of five brothers who became prominent in the sports world.

Elizabeth Rorty

Someone once asked if Elizabeth Rorty had ever married and was told she hadn't. "Oh, yes, she did," replied a bystander. "She was married to harness racing." That's an apt description of the Goshen native who was one of the sport's foremost journalists in the post–World War II era. She became managing editor of the *Horseman & Fair World*, and her weekly "Down the Stretch" column was filled with insights and humor.

Rorty and her sidekick Frances Wallace were so impressed by The Intruder's fastest workout before the 1956 Hambletonian that they badgered owner Leonard Buck into starting him in the big race. The Intruder had won only one time in his life but came away a surprise winner in the Hambletonian.

Known to her friends simply as "Weed" (a childhood nickname), Rorty was respected and liked by horsemen in an era when women were invisible in the sport. She witnessed forty-four of the fifty-one Hambletonians raced during her lifetime and was a parade marshal three times. She died in 1977 in Lexington.

William Rysdyk

A decision made when he was a young farmhand changed William Rysdyk's life, giving him immortality and making him a rich man. He was a young man working on the farm of Jonas Seeley when he took a shine to a robust bay colt out of a crippled mare. He managed to come up with $125 to purchase the colt from Seeley and named him Hambletonian.

The horse was thereafter known as Rysdyk's Hambletonian or Hambletonian 10, and he began breeding service at age two. His offspring gained popularity with horse owners, and his blood soon came to dominate the trotting world. Rysdyk was fortunate that Hambletonian was a fertile horse and able to handle the large number of mares sent to him, making Rysdyk wealthy beyond his imagination.

George Segal

Segal grew up on Long Island and became a fan of racing by attending the races at Roosevelt Raceway, like so many others who became breeders and owners. He relocated to Chicago and achieved success on the commodities market.

A History of Trotters, Tracks and Horsemen

Known for having exquisite taste in his horseflesh, Segal owned some of the most influential stallions in harness racing. Western Hanover, Artsplace and Life Sign concurrently stood at stud, and all were Segal horses. He also owned the superb pacing fillies Three Diamonds (dam of Life Sign) and Leah Almahurst (dam of Western Ideal).

Segal was a student of pedigrees and relied on his primary trainer, Gene Riegle, to evaluate conformation. The Segal/Riegle team operated with extraordinary success at the top of the sport.

Segal owned many horses in partnership and operated Brittany Farms in Versailles, Kentucky, which annually sent a consignment of blue-blood trotting and pacing yearlings to the yearling auctions.

JOHN SPLAN

Born in Little Falls in 1849, Splan raced many high-class trotters in the late 1800s, including the champion Rarus and the pacer Johnston. After a successful career on the track, he switched to working with sale companies and as an advisor for Walnut Hall Farm. His book *Life with the Trotters* (1889) is still considered a classic.

LELAND STANFORD

Although he is associated with California, where a highly regarded university bears his name, Stanford was, in fact, a native New Yorker, born near Albany in 1824. He went west at age twenty-six and ultimately became governor of California. He established Palo Alto Stock Farm, where he bred many champions. In 1877, he purchased Electioneer, a son of Hambletonian, from Stony Ford Farm in Campbell Hall, New York. Electioneer became a major sire, and his line is now the breed's dominant pacing male line.

CHARLES "DOC" TANNER

Born in 1865, the final year of the Civil War, Tanner tried varied jobs before becoming affiliated with Walnut Grove Farm in Washingtonville, New York. He then established himself as a trainer of matinee horses for wealthy owners. His most famous patron was C.K.G. Billings, and Tanner trained his stable and exhibited the champion trotters Lou Dillon and Uhlan.

BETTY WEHLE

Wehle was a pioneer woman in the breeding of Standardbreds in New York. She and her husband, Jack, whose family owned the Genesee Brewing Company, had a large farm near Rochester. She enjoyed great success as a young woman campaigning Yankee Hanover and later standing him as a stallion at her farm. His success on the track made Wehle into a lifelong horsewoman.

Other stallions that took up residence at the Wehles' farm were Gold Worthy, the 1974 Hambletonian winner Christopher T and the fast pacer Cory. Wehle was a major force in establishing the New York Sire Stakes in the 1960s and was also active in the Harness Horse Breeders of New York.

She died in 2004 at age eighty-two.

Charles W. Williams

His connection to New York was brief. Born in Chatham County in 1856, he moved to Iowa when he was a youngster. As an adult, he loved trotters and sent two mares to Kentucky to be bred in 1885. They produced the colts Axtell and Allerton. Axtell was sold to a syndicate for $105,000, and Allerton was so great that Williams rejected an offer of $150,000. He took his profits from Axtell and ploughed them into a revolutionary kite-shaped track at Independence, Iowa.

The track and the race meetings held there were all the rage in the late 1800s and early 1900s, and Williams was a prominent figure in harness racing. He left the horse business in 1908 and spent almost three decades as a traveling evangelist.

Frank Wiswall

This robust attorney from Upstate New York was the ultimate insider, a man whose role in establishing the United State Trotting Association and parimutuel harness racing in his native state was best appreciated by those far from public view.

If Roland Harriman is the man who amalgamated the divergent parties into the United State Trotting Association, Frank Wiswall was the man who made the new organization work. Wiswall virtually wrote the USTA rulebook single-handedly in one weekend, with only minor changes later.

Wiswall was a successful and respected attorney in New York, but he had to travel across the country to sell the USTA to horsemen in remote locations. Overcoming their opposition wasn't always easy, but Wiswall could be a very convincing man. His father was a veterinarian, and Frank graduated from Albany Law School. He was admitted to the New York Bar in 1917, did service in France during World War I and then returned to be elected to the New York State Assembly at age twenty-four in 1919. The following year, he was elected to the state senate.

In 1940, Wiswall was named secretary of the New York State Harness Racing Commission and helped to draft the rules for racing in the Empire State. He was also involved in the ownership and construction of Saratoga Raceway and, in fact, drove his pacer Friscowyn to victory on opening night at Saratoga. He continued his interests in Saratoga after resigning as secretary of the State Harness Racing Commission in 1945. He then opened Runnymede Farm and took great pride in his racing and breeding operation.

Wiswall died at age seventy-seven in 1972.

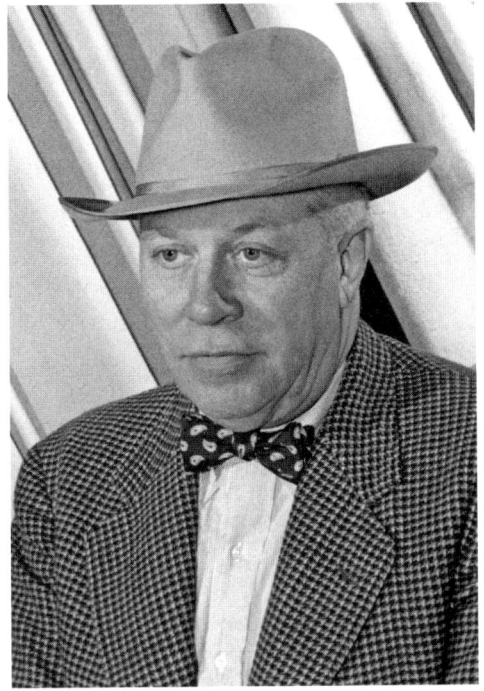

Frank Wiswall was the man who wrote the rulebook for the U.S. Trotting Association practically on his own and then convinced horsemen how essential the association was for racing's growth. He was an Upstate New York lawyer with a deft political touch and a fondness for horses.

NORMAN S. WOOLWORTH

Woolworth was born in New York City at a time when the Woolworth Building was the tallest building in the world. He had an avid interest in sports and started owning Standardbreds in the early 1950s. He personally selected the trotting filly Egyptian Princess and enjoyed watching her splendid career. He even took her to race in the Prix d'Amerique in France, sparking an interest in international competition that lasted the rest of his life.

Woolworth purchased the sophomore pacing colt Meadow Skipper in 1963 and turned him over to trainer Earle Avery. The tall brown colt was a remarkable racehorse and a stallion of extraordinary influence. He stood at Stoner Creek Stud in Kentucky, which Woolworth owned in partnership with his longtime friend David Johnston.

Woolworth bred and raced many champions under the name of his Clearview Stable. Included among them were Maxine's Dream, Muncy Hanover, Porterhouse, Gun Runner, Zoot Suit, French Chef, Smokin Yankee and others. He realized a lifetime dream when his homebred filly Duenna won the Hambletonian in 1983.

Later in his life, Woolworth took an avid interest in Swedish trotting, maintaining broodmares and a few racehorses there. He died in 2003.

THEODORE J. ZORNOW

Zornow served as president of the United State Trotting Association in the 1970s and was also vice-president and director of the Harness Horse Breeders of New York. In addition, he was a director of the Hall of Fame and Hambletonian Society.

Zornow was a 1929 graduate of the University of Rochester and owner of Pittsford Flour Mills Inc. and T.J. Zornow Inc. He served as president of the New York State Grain & Bean Shippers Assocation and many other industry organizations. He owned and operated Avon Farms and was associated with such top-flight horses as Tar Boy, Kat Byrd, Maynard Hanover, Anthony Hanover, Concho Hanover, Kathena and Munger Hanover. Levi Harner trained his horses for many years.

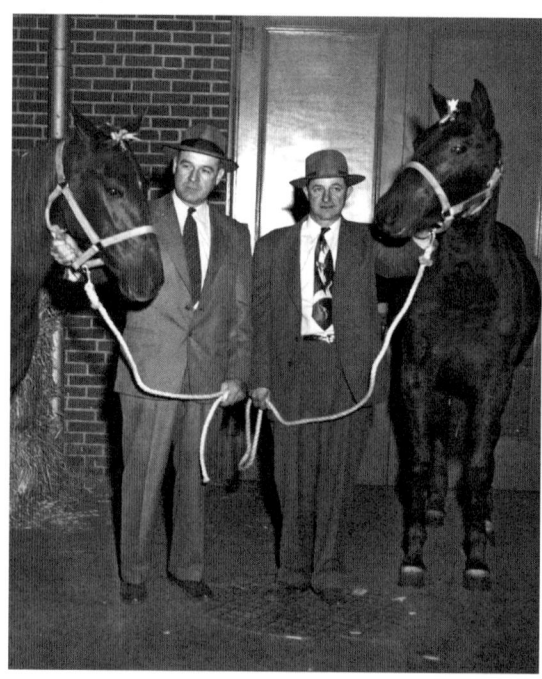

Ted Zornow (left) and Levi Harner campaigned a potent stable in New York for many years. Zornow operated Avon Farms in western New York and served as president of the U.S. Trotting Association. Harner's accomplishments won him Hall of Fame honors.

HARRY M. ZWEIG

Often considered the father of the New York Sire Stakes, this veterinarian was a native of New York City and a graduate of Ohio State University. He practiced in Nassau near Albany for thirty-eight years. Zweig was instrumental in passing the Laverne Law in New York that led to tremendous growth in funding for New York racing. He was president of the Harness Horse Breeders of New York and operated Middlebrook Farms. He led the revival of racing at the New York State Fair and is honored today by the Dr. Harry M. Zweig Memorial Trot.

Sources

Every person who attempts to write about the history of harness racing owes a special debt to John L. Hervey, author of the monumental classic *The American Trotter*, published just before Hervey's passing at the end of 1947. Hervey had personal knowledge of harness racing starting from the last decade of the nineteenth century until almost the midpoint of the twentieth century. Perhaps more significantly, Hervey had a passion for recording the history of the breed in the early years of the sport. I have drawn from Hervey's writings, as I have long found them as reliable as they are captivating.

Articles from the Standardbred trade journals such as now defunct *Harness Horse*, the *Horseman & Fair World* and *Hoof Beats* provided valuable information. Press guides from tracks such as Yonkers Raceway and Roosevelt Raceway proved help, as did the *Trotting & Pacing Guide*. A history of Batavia Downs by Bill Brown was useful, as was *The Complete Book of Harness Racing* by Phil Pines.

About the Author

Dean Hoffman is a native of Cincinnati and a graduate of Ohio University's School of Journalism. He worked in various public relations and advertising positions before being named executive editor of *Hoof Beats*, the official publication of the U.S. Trotting Association. He held that position for twenty-five years and received numerous honors, including induction into the Harness Racing Hall of Fame Communicators Corner. He also won the Messenger Award, the highest honor bestowed by Harness Tracks of America. He has traveled extensively to harness tracks in Sweden, Australia, Russia, Norway, England, France, Finland, Germany and other countries. He is the author of four previous books on harness racing.

Visit us at
www.historypress.net